Making Sense
of the Book
of Revelation

OTHER BOOKS BY ROBERT L. MILLET

Making Sense
of the Book
of Revelation

Robert L. Millet

DESERET
BOOK

SALT LAKE CITY, UTAH

Library of Congress Cataloging-in-Publication Data
Millet, Robert L. author.
  Making sense of the book of Revelation / Robert L. Millet.
    pages cm
  Includes bibliographical references and index.
  ISBN 978-1-60641-944-1 (paperbound)
  1. Bible. N.T. Revelation—Criticism, interpretation, etc. 2. Eschatology. 3. The Church of Jesus Christ of Latter-day Saints—Doctrines. I. Title.
  BS2825.52.M555 2011
  228'.06—dc22   2011007161

Printed in the United States of America
Worzalla Publishing Co., Stevens Point, WI

10 9 8 7 6 5 4 3 2 1

CONTENTS

Introduction

MAKING SENSE OF JOHN'S REVELATION

Perhaps no book of scripture has led to more speculation, spawned more foolishness, and resulted in more spiritual imbalance than the Apocalypse—the Revelation of John the Beloved. It was an important book in the first century of the Christian era, one that provided hope and perspective for the former-day Saints. And, when properly approached and understood, it provides a like hope for Latter-day Saints who live in the twenty-first century. Although it is not likely that even the most serious students of scripture will uncover every symbol and thereby come to understand every particular of the Revelation, there are certain doctrinal refrains, recurring lessons, and basic principles that may be grasped by all of us.

Background

The author of Revelation is John, the brother of James and son of Zebedee. This is the same John who served as an Apostle and a leader of the meridian Church and who wrote the Gospel of John and the three epistles. He is known variously as John the Beloved, John the Revelator, and the one Jesus loved (John 21:20). We know from the Book of Mormon (3 Nephi 28:6–7) and from modern revelation (D&C 7) that John was translated—changed

1

to a terrestrial state in which he would no longer be subject to the effects of the Fall, including physical suffering, bodily decay, and death. Like the three Nephites, he is still ministering among the people of the earth and will do so until the Second Coming of Jesus Christ, at which time he and they will be changed from mortality to immortality (3 Nephi 28:8, 27–30).[1] This book of scripture is called "The Revelation of John, a servant of God, which was given unto him of Jesus Christ" (JST, Revelation 1:1).

Though many modern biblical scholars are prone to cast doubt on the authorship of John the Beloved, his authorship has been attested from as early as the second century A.D. by Justin Martyr. The actual time of the writing is unknown, and debates continue among New Testament scholars. Some date the *Apocalypse*, a Greek work meaning revelation or unveiling, during the reign of the Roman emperor Domitian (A.D. 81–96), while others propose a date some time during the reign of Vespasian (A.D. 69–79). What we do know is that John wrote this book from the island of Patmos (see Revelation 1:9), a small volcanic island just southwest of Ephesus. The Revelation contains specific counsel, condemnation, warning, and prophetic promises to the seven churches of Asia—Ephesus, Smyrna, Pergamos, Thyatira, Sardis, Philadelphia, and Laodicea—branches of the Christian Church that had been organized by the Apostle Paul during his missionary journeys.

Apocalyptic Literature

As most readers of Revelation can attest, reading this book is unlike any other experience in scripture. Whereas most of the Book of Mormon, for example, is given to us "in plainness" (2 Nephi 25:4; 31:3; 33:6), Revelation is not terribly plain to the generality of Saints. John's messages are not always clear, and coming to understand what is intended often requires extensive cross-referencing, searching out historical details, and much pondering and discernment. It does not help that "many plain and precious" truths have been taken from the Bible (1 Nephi 13:20–40), and specifically from Revelation.

Nephi was given a panoramic vision, a view of things from beginning to end (1 Nephi 11–14). He was told, however, that he would not be permitted to write the whole of the vision in the Nephite record but that another, the Apostle John, would be asked to do so. "Wherefore, the things which he shall write are just and true; and behold they are written in the book which thou beheld proceeding out of the mouth of the Jew; and at the time they proceeded out of the mouth of the Jew, or, at the time the book proceeded out of the mouth of the Jew, the things which were written were plain and pure, and most precious and easy to the understanding of all men" (1 Nephi 14:21–23).

Like Lehi's dream or vision and in Nephi's vision, John's revelation was a God's-eye view of things from eternity past to eternity future. "John had the curtains of heaven withdrawn," the Prophet Joseph Smith explained, "and by vision looked through the dark vista of future ages, and contemplated events that should transpire throughout every subsequent period of time, until the final winding up scene."[2] John's book is an example of apocalyptic literature. Other examples of apocalyptic literature include chapters in Ezekiel and Daniel, Matthew 24 (sometimes called the "little Apocalypse"), Mark 13, and 1 Nephi 13–14. These all contain some apocalyptic elements. Chronology seems irrelevant in apocalyptic writing. The writer seems to jump back and forth through time, darting from distant past to distant future in the blink of an eye. Thus we read of two prophets in Revelation 11 who will be killed at the time of the battle of Armageddon for their testimony and then discover the war in heaven in Revelation 12. To God, for whom the past, the present, and the future are "one eternal 'now'"[3] time is not reckoned in the same way.

The following are additional elements and characteristics of apocalyptic writings (Revelation contains all of these):

1. *Symbols.* This literary genre is filled with symbols—objects or messages that represent or typify other things. We find in Revelation such figures as lambs, dragons, candlesticks, stars, white stones, a sea of glass, animals filled with eyes and wings, books with seals, a bottomless pit, a huge cubic city, trumpets, vials with bitter potions, various-colored horses, white robes, seals on the forehead or right hand, locusts and scorpions, little books that are eaten, olive trees, a great whore, and a tree with "twelve manner of fruits" (Revelation 22:2). These all point to greater realities and deeper messages. They are symbols. In some cases we are able to uncover the symbolism through a careful reading of Revelation itself, but frequently we must turn to other revelation (particularly modern revelation) to uncover the meaning. And in some cases we are left without scriptural or prophetic commentary.

2. *Beasts.* There are many types of beasts in Revelation, and some of these are easier to understand than others. The Prophet Joseph Smith explained: "It is not very essential for the elders to have knowledge in relation to the meaning of beasts, and heads and horns, and other figures made use of in the revelations. . . .

"I make this broad declaration, that whenever God gives a vision of an image, or beast, or figure of any kind, He always holds Himself responsible to give a revelation or interpretation of the meaning thereof, otherwise we are not responsible or accountable for our belief in it. Don't be afraid of being damned for not knowing the meaning of a vision or figure, if God has not given a revelation or interpretation of the subject."[4]

3. *Numbers.* It is common in apocalyptic writings to find numbers everywhere—three, seven, twelve, and forty. The number seven, for example, which represents wholeness or perfection in Greek, occurs fifty-two times in Revelation; everything in

Revelation seems to be done in sevens—for instance, seven seals (5:1–8:5), seven trumpets (8:6–11:19), seven significant signs (12:1–14:20), and seven last plagues (15:1–16:21).

4. *Astral phenomena.* Often we read of things taking place in the heavens as well as on the earth—stars falling, the heavens being shaken, the moon turning to blood, a burning fire from heaven hitting the earth, and so forth. These signs and symbols seem to represent unrest in the universe, God's anger, or the coming destruction of the wicked.

5. *Cosmic dualism.* In apocalyptic literature the world is a battleground between light and darkness, good and evil, the kingdom of God and the kingdom of the devil. Satan rules and reigns now in a fallen world, but the time is not far distant when the God of heaven will step into history, defeat the powers of darkness, and bring to an end all wickedness on earth. Today may be the day of Lucifer's power, but the future belongs to Jehovah. Thus the plea of Revelation to the true and faithful on earth is essentially "Hold on! The day of the Lord is at hand. Don't give up, don't give in, don't compromise or concede to diabolical forces; the time of deliverance is near."

Some Guides to Interpretation

First, there is no substitute for reading Revelation straight through, looking for key themes and seeking to understand the grand overarching and undergirding messages of the book. It is worth our while to read Revelation several times to simply recognize the doctrinal refrains and recurring precepts that John chose to weave through this remarkable document. The big picture is crucial. As the Prophet Joseph Smith suggested, it probably doesn't matter a great deal whether we know exactly what this beast, that horn, or some poisonous vial represents; but it does matter whether we get the point of the book.

Second, to paraphrase Nephi, the book of Revelation, though a sealed book to many, is clear to those who have "the spirit of prophecy" (2 Nephi 25:4). There is absolutely no way for us to grasp what John intended unless we are moved upon by the same Spirit that moved upon the Revelator. That is to say, it takes revelation to understand Revelation. The spirit of prophecy, which is the spirit of revelation—the same spirit that plants within our souls "the testimony of Jesus" (Revelation 19:10)—will lead us unto that level of understanding the Lord intends for each of us.

Third, the greatest commentary on scripture is scripture. Indeed, the best way to understand Revelation is to rely on other books of scripture, particularly the scriptures of the Restoration. President Marion G. Romney emphatically stressed the need to search and study modern revelation. He declared: "In each dispensation . . . the Lord has revealed anew the principles of the gospel. So that while the records of past dispensations, insofar as they are uncorrupted, testify to the truths of the gospel, still each dispensation has had revealed in its day sufficient truth to guide the people of the new dispensation, independent of the records of the past.

"I do not wish to discredit in any manner the records we have of the truths revealed by the Lord in past dispensations. What I now desire is to impress upon our minds that the gospel, as revealed to the Prophet Joseph Smith, is complete and is the word direct from heaven to this dispensation. It alone is sufficient to teach us the principles of eternal life. It is the truth revealed, the commandments given in this dispensation through modern prophets by which we are to be governed."[5]

For example, certain sections of the Doctrine and Covenants (29, 45, 77, 84, 88, 133) provide invaluable insight into John's work. Section 77 is especially helpful; it explains details concerning people and events in Revelation 4, 5, 7, 8, 9, 10, and 11. First Nephi 13–14 and Ether 4 and 13 in the Book of Mormon are also instructive. Joseph Smith's translation of the Bible is an indispensable aid; under inspiration, the Prophet altered 20 percent of the book of Revelation (including about 95 percent of Revelation 12). Finally, a sermon delivered by the Prophet on April 8, 1843, in Nauvoo contains several valuable insights regarding Revelation.[6]

One other guiding principle may be useful. The Prophet Joseph explained, "The things which John saw had no allusion to the scenes of the days of Adam, Enoch, Abraham or Jesus, *only so far as is plainly represented by John, and clearly set forth by him.* John saw that only which was lying in futurity and which was shortly to come to pass."[7] The first three chapters of Revelation are directed to the seven churches of Asia and address problems current in John's day—problems of conversion, immorality, idolatry, and apostasy in general. In addition, other than a brief glimpse into the past in the first eleven verses of Revelation 6, in which John reviews the history of the world from the beginning to the meridian dispensation,[8] Revelation deals with "things which must be hereafter" (Revelation 4:1). To put this in perspective, only eleven verses discuss the events of the first five seals, meaning the period of time from the Creation to A.D. 1000. This is approximately 3 percent of the total number of verses in Revelation. On the other hand, 281 verses, or about 70 percent, deal with the sixth and seventh seals, the period of time from A.D. 1000 to the end of the Millennium.

Part One

EXAMINING THE BOOK
OF REVELATION

1

PROLOGUE (1:1–20)

Revelation 1

Revelation 1 is John's explanation of the revelation given to him. It is "the Revelation of John, a servant of God, which was given unto him of Jesus Christ" (JST, Revelation 1:1), showing forth "things which must shortly come to pass." This vision came from him "which is, and which was, and which is to come" (v. 4)*. The early elders of this dispensation were commanded to "bear record of me, even Jesus Christ, that I am the Son of the living God, that I was, that I am, and that I am to come" (D&C 68:6). Joseph Smith explained, "The great Jehovah contemplated the whole of the events connected with the earth, pertaining to the plan of salvation, before it rolled into existence, or ever 'the morning stars sang together' for joy; *the past, the present, and the future were and are, with Him, one eternal 'now.'*"[1]

John received this marvelous manifestation while he was in the Spirit on the Lord's day, "the first day of the week" (Acts 20:7). Now a senior Apostle, John is by order of the Roman emperor in

---

* In this and all further parenthetical references to verse numbers without book or chapter, the chapter is understood to be the chapter of Revelation under discussion; e.g., verse 4 in this reference is to Revelation 1:4.

11

exile on the island of Patmos, a small landmass off the coast of Asia Minor (present-day Turkey), about sixty miles southwest of Ephesus. He is given a strict charge to write the vision and send it to seven specific branches of the Church in Asia: Ephesus, Smyrna, Pergamos, Thyatira, Sardis, Philadelphia, and Laodicea. Presumably these branches had been organized by the Apostle Paul during his ministry as the Apostle to the Gentiles.

As the Savior speaks to John, The Beloved Apostle turns toward the source of the voice (v. 12; see 3 Nephi 11:3–6). Upon doing so, he sees seven golden candlesticks, representing the seven churches, and the Lord Jesus in all his glory, standing in the midst of the churches and clothed "with a garment down to the foot, and girt about the paps with a golden girdle" (v. 13). Note the marvelous description given of the risen Lord: "His head and his hairs were white like wool, as white as snow; and his eyes were as a flame of fire; and his feet like unto fine brass, as if they burned in a furnace; and his voice as the sound of many waters" (vv. 14–15). That same Lord appeared eighteen centuries later to Joseph Smith and Oliver Cowdery in the Kirtland Temple. They declared:

"We saw the Lord standing upon the breastwork of the pulpit, before us; and under his feet was a paved work of pure gold, in color like amber. His eyes were as a flame of fire; the hair of his head was white like the pure snow; his countenance shone above the brightness of the sun; and his voice was as the sound of the rushing of great waters, even the voice of Jehovah, saying: I am the first and the last [see Isaiah 48:12]; I am he who liveth, I am he who was slain; I am your advocate with the Father" (D&C 110:2–4). Christ stands, holding seven stars, or the seven servants (JST, Revelation 1:20)—legal administrators within the priesthood, bishops and other leaders of the seven churches of Asia.

Out of the Lord's mouth "went a sharp two edged sword" (v. 16). In modern revelation the Savior has counseled repeatedly,

"Behold, I am God; give heed unto my word, which is quick and powerful, sharper than a two-edged sword, to the dividing asunder of both joints and marrow; therefore give heed unto my words" (D&C 6:2; see also 11:2; 12:2; 14:2). Mormon taught that "whosoever will may lay hold upon the word of God, which is quick [alive, lively] and powerful, which shall divide asunder all the cunning and the snares and the wiles of the devil, and lead the man of Christ in a strait and narrow course across that everlasting gulf of misery which is prepared to engulf the wicked—and land their souls, yea, their immortal souls, at the right hand of God in the kingdom of heaven, to sit down with Abraham, and Isaac, and with Jacob, and with all our holy fathers, to go no more out" (Helaman 3:29–30).

He who was slain and yet who lives, he who won the victory over the grave and came forth unto glorious immortality and eternal life, proclaimed to John, "I am he that liveth, and was dead; and, behold, I am alive for evermore, Amen; and have the keys of hell and of death" (v. 18). "His kingdom cannot fail," we sing in adoration, "He rules o'er earth and heav'n. / The keys of death and hell / To Christ the Lord are giv'n."

> *Lift up your heart!*
> *Lift up your voice!*
> *Rejoice, again I say, rejoice!*[2]

2

THE LETTERS TO THE CHURCHES (2:1–3:22)

Revelation 2

Revelation 2 begins with specific counsel to the church at Ephesus, written particularly to the priesthood leader or servant of the church (see JST, Revelation 2:1). The Lord first commends the Saints for their ability to discern and try the false apostles who had attempted to deceive the believers (v. 2; see also D&C 64:37–39). The Saints at Ephesus have "borne, and [have] patience, and for my name's sake [have] laboured, and [have] not fainted" (v. 3). To their credit, they hate "the deeds of the Nicolaitans" (v. 6), which will be discussed shortly.

Nevertheless, the Ephesians are reproved for faulty priorities, for having "left [their] first love," the way of total consecration to the Lord and his Church (v. 4). "To love God with all your heart, soul, mind, and strength," President Ezra Taft Benson declared, "is all-consuming and all-encompassing. . . . The breadth, depth, and height of this love of God extend into every facet of one's life. Our desires, be they spiritual or temporal, should be rooted in a love of the Lord." Further, "We must put God in the forefront of everything else in our lives. He must come first. . . .

"When we put God first, all other things fall into their proper place or drop out of our lives. Our love of the Lord will govern the claims for our affection, the demands on our time, the interests we pursue, and the order of our priorities."[1]

If the Saints at Ephesus are not careful, Christ warns, he will remove his Church from among them, and they will forfeit the blessings of the gospel of Jesus Christ. On the other hand, if they hold out faithful and overcome the world, to them it will be given "to eat of the tree of life, which is in the midst of the paradise of God" (v. 7). In other words, they will partake everlastingly of eternal life and exaltation; they will inherit the highest heaven hereafter. "Come unto me and ye shall partake of the fruit of the tree of life; yea, ye shall eat and drink of the bread and the waters of life freely" (Alma 5:34; see also 32:39–42; John 4:13–14; 6:27; 7:37).

The Lord next addresses the servant of the church at Smyrna. "I know thy works, and tribulation, and poverty, (but thou art rich)" (v. 9). It is not uncommon for the Saints of the Most High to be poor as pertaining to the things of this world, to work and labor and struggle to make ends meet. And yet, there is a sacred supplement that comes to the faithful, an outpouring of joy and peace and love and gratitude, an endowment of the Spirit that cannot be counted in currency. "Seek not for riches but for wisdom," the Lord said in April 1829, "and behold, the mysteries of God shall be unfolded unto you" (D&C 6:7). The heavens will be opened, the veil will be thin, and the earnest seeker after truth will come to know things that cannot be known by the worldly or the wayward, things that can be comprehended only by the power of the Spirit; these are the mysteries of God.[2] The revelation continues: "And then shall you be made rich. Behold, he that hath eternal life is rich" (D&C 6:7). "And if ye seek the riches which it is the will of the Father to give unto you, ye shall be the richest of all people, for ye shall have the riches of eternity" (D&C 38:39).

The Master expresses his awareness of "the blasphemy of them which say they are Jews, and are not, but are the synagogue of

Satan" (v. 9). These are no doubt Jews at Smyrna and elsewhere in the empire who were hostile toward the Christians, perhaps providing the Romans with details that could lead to arrest and even death. The Saints may be called upon to suffer pain and persecution and prison, tribulation and testing, betrayal and even death for the cause of Christ. "Be thou faithful unto death, and I will give thee a crown of life" (v. 10). The Saints are counseled not to fear (nor to take counsel from their fears) but to endure and overcome so that they will "not be hurt of the second death" (v. 11)— spiritual death, the final spiritual separation of man from God (see Alma 12:16; 42:9; Helaman 14:18; D&C 29:41).

The Saints at Pergamos are commended for standing fast in the faith in a city that is the center of the state religion at Rome (v. 13), a place in which emperor worship was expected. The Lord cautions the members against those amongst them who "hold the doctrine of Balaam" (v. 14) or, in other words, pervert the right ways of the Lord for monetary benefit (see Numbers 22:5; 2 Peter 2:15). The people at Pergamos are chastened for holding to the doctrine of the Nicolaitans. Elder Bruce R. McConkie speaks generally of the Nicolaitans as "members of the Church who were trying to maintain their church standing while continuing to live after the manner of the world. They must have had some specific doctrinal teachings which they used to justify their course."[3] In addition, "The Nicolaitans appear to have gnostic tendencies. . . . Their teaching could have been based on a dualism claiming that what was done in the body had no bearing on the soul."[4] Bishop Irenaus taught that the Nicolaitans were a heretical group who followed Nicolaus, one of the seven men chosen as special assistants to the Twelve in Acts 6:5.[5] In a revelation given in July 1838, Bishop Newel K. Whitney was chastised for his "littleness of soul" and shamed for his involvement with a "Nicolaitane band"; in this case, Brother Whitney had remained in Kirtland with William Marks in order to capitalize on the sale of property and had hesitated to join the Saints in Missouri (D&C 117:11).

Those who overcome are promised the privilege of eating of the "hidden manna" (v. 17), or the fruit of the tree of life. In addition, all "who overcome by faith" (D&C 76:53; see also 76:60) and thus inherit celestial glory will be given a "white stone, and in the stone a new name written, which no man knoweth saving he that receiveth it" (v. 17). This white stone, which will become a Urim and Thummim to each celestial candidate, will reveal things pertaining to the celestial order of things (D&C 130:10–11).

Jesus expresses his pleasure in the fact that the members of the church at Thyatira have been examples of charity, service, faith, and patience (vv. 18–19). Praise is followed swiftly by rebuke, however, because they allowed Jezebel, a false prophetess and teacher of Balaamism, to deceive and seduce the Saints into degradation. The Lord grants unto her a probationary period of repentance that, if not wisely used, will be followed by stern divine judgment: Jezebel and her cohorts in corruption are to be cast into hell (vv. 20–23). To those who overcome and keep the commandments will be given kingly authority in the resurrection, even "power over many kingdoms" (JST, Revelation 2:26). Such a people will receive, in John's words, "the morning star" (v. 28). Perhaps this is related to what Peter referred to as the "day star" (2 Peter 1:19), or "more sure word of prophecy" (D&C 131:5–6). Jesus later identifies himself as "the root and the offspring of David, and the bright and morning star" (Revelation 22:16).

Revelation 3

The Saints at Sardis are reprimanded for letting their spiritual guards down and descending into a state of wickedness. Though the church at Sardis had for many years enjoyed "a name" (v. 1), meaning an excellent reputation for righteousness, they had fallen, on the whole, into spiritual death. The Savior declared, "I have not found thy works perfect before God" (v. 2), meaning the people were not "perfect in Christ" (Moroni 10:32). Rather than being spiritually mature, whole or complete, filled with integrity, their eye was not single; their lives were fragmented, not given wholly to the Lord and his work and glory. Thus they are admonished to watch and pray, never knowing when (1) any of them might die and come face-to-face with God; or (2) the Lord will return in power and great glory. The King of kings will come in glory, but he will come to the unprepared and the worldly "as a thief in the night" (1 Thessalonians 5:2; D&C 106:4; see also v. 3). The priesthood leader at Sardis is reminded that there are yet a few in his city who "have not defiled their garments" or broken their eternal covenants. These "shall walk with me in white: for they are worthy" (v. 4), having had their garments washed white in the blood of the Lamb. The Lord will not blot out their names from his book of life, "the record which is kept in heaven" (D&C 128:7), even "the book of the names of the sanctified" (D&C 88:2).

Next the Savior addresses the members at Philadelphia. "These things saith he that is holy, he that is true, he that hath the key of David, he that openeth, and no man shutteth; and shutteth, and no man openeth" (v. 7). Elder Bruce R. McConkie wrote: "In ancient Israel, David was a man of blood and battle whose word was law and whose very name was also a symbol of power and authority. Accordingly, when Isaiah sought to convey a realization of the supreme, directive control and power resident in our Lord, the Son of David, he spoke these words in the Lord's name: 'And *the key of the house of David* will I lay upon his shoulder; so he shall open, and none shall shut; and he shall shut, and none shall open.' (Isa. 22:22.) . . . Thus, the *key of David* is the absolute power resident in Christ whereby his will is expressed in all things both temporal and spiritual."[6] No power on earth or in hell can disannul the commendation and blessing of the Savior, and similarly no force or authority anywhere can prevent the mighty Messiah from pronouncing judgment and condemnation upon the ungodly.

These believers are praised for faithfulness and strength, especially in a city containing another "synagogue of Satan" (v. 9). Because of such dedication, the Saints are promised the following: (1) those wicked Jews who reject Christ and his gospel will eventually be forced to bow down before those possessing the truth, and they will know and acknowledge that the Saints were the chosen of God (see v. 9); (2) because of their faith the Lord will deliver the Saints from trials and temptations that engulf the wicked (see v. 10); (3) they will become "a pillar in the temple of my God" (v. 12), a man or woman of faith, of substance, and of righteous influence; (4) the Lord promises to "write upon [them] the name of my God, . . . and I will write upon [them] my new name" (v. 12). To receive the name of God is to become the sons and daughters of God, to become heirs of God and joint heirs with Jesus Christ. It is to inherit the fulness of the Father, to inherit with Christ the Firstborn as though we were the firstborn; it is to qualify for membership in what the scriptures call "the church of the Firstborn" (D&C 76:54, 94; 93:22; see also 76:67).

The final church to receive specific commandment, Laodicea, receives a fiery condemnation from the Master for its "lukewarm" approach to gospel living (vv. 14–16). "So then," says Christ, "because thou art lukewarm, and neither cold nor hot, I will spue [vomit] thee out of my mouth" (v. 16). Such is in store for "good, upright, decent members of the Church who nonetheless do not put first in their lives the things of God's earthly kingdom. They have testimonies; they know the work is true; but they specialize, as it were, in the social gospel; that is, in that portion of the truth which seems to bless others on pretty much the same basis as people are bettered by any good concepts in any church."[7] In other words, "these are they who are not valiant in the testimony of Jesus; wherefore, they obtain not the crown over the kingdom of our God" and will thus inherit a terrestrial glory (D&C 76:79–80).

The Laodiceans are counseled to lay aside the things of this world for the things of a better; to seek the purest gold (see v. 18), even the gold that Jesus Christ gives; to seek "the greatest of all the gifts of God"—eternal life (D&C 6:13; 14:7); to clothe themselves in "white raiment," the robes of righteousness; and to anoint their eyes with the sanctifying salve of the Holy Spirit (v. 18). Then comes the well-known and comforting assurance and sacred invitation: "Behold, I stand at the door, and knock: if any man hear my voice, and open the door, I will come in to him, and will sup with him, and he with me" (v. 20). Those who strive through the enabling power of Christ to put off their fallen nature are promised that they will sit with Christ in his throne, even as he (who overcame) sits now at his Father's throne (v. 21); they are glorified in Christ as he is in the Father (D&C 93:20).

3

A VISION OF HEAVEN (4:1–11)

Revelation 4

Revelation 4 begins another division of the revelation to John—a vision of "things which must be hereafter" (v. 1). The Revelator is permitted to gaze into heaven and behold the eternal throne of God the Father. John sees twenty-four elders seated around the holy throne, "clothed in white raiment; and they had on their heads crowns of gold" (v. 4). We learn from modern revelation that "these elders whom John saw, were elders who had been faithful in the work of the ministry and were dead; who belonged to the seven churches, and were then in the paradise of God" (D&C 77:5).

Next, before his eyes and amidst the thundering and lightning surrounding the glory of God, John sees the seven priesthood leaders of the churches standing before the throne of God (see v. 5). He was privileged to see, before the throne, "a sea of glass like unto crystal" (v. 6), representing "the earth, in its sanctified, immortal, and eternal state" (D&C 77:1). Joseph Smith taught, "This earth, in its sanctified and immortal state, will be made like unto crystal and will be a Urim and Thummim to the inhabitants who dwell thereon, whereby all things pertaining to an inferior kingdom, or all kingdoms of a lower order, will be manifest to those who dwell on it; and this earth will be Christ's" (D&C 130:9).

Also surrounding the throne of God were four beasts, each with six wings (v. 8) and "full of eyes before and behind" (v. 6). The wings represent power (to move, to act, and so forth), while the eyes symbolize the fact that the beasts are exalted and thus filled with "light and knowledge" (see D&C 77:4). What are the four beasts? They are actual creatures John saw in heaven, but they represent the fact that all creatures will be resurrected from the dead unto "the enjoyment of their eternal felicity" (D&C 77:3). In addition, "the four beasts," wrote the Prophet Joseph, "were four of the most noble animals that had filled the measure of their creation, and had been saved from other worlds, because they were perfect: they were like angels in their sphere. We are not told where they came from, and I do not know; but they were seen and heard by John praising and glorifying God."[1] These beasts join with the twenty-four elders in shouting praise and adoration to the Father: "Thou art worthy, O Lord, to receive glory and honour and power: for thou hast created all things, and for thy pleasure they are and were created" (v. 11).

4

THE SEVEN SEALS (5:1–8:5)

Revelation 5

The Revelator then notices that God the Father has within his right hand a book, literally a scroll, written on both sides and containing seven seals so that only a portion of the scroll could be unrolled at a time (see v. 1). This book or scroll "contains the revealed will, mysteries, and the works of God; the hidden things of his economy concerning this earth during the seven thousand years of its continuance, or its temporal existence" (D&C 77:6). Further, "the first seal contains the things of the first thousand years, and the second also of the second thousand years, and so on until the seventh" (D&C 77:7). A question seems now to reverberate through the heavens: Who is worthy to open the book and loose the seals? (see v. 2). Who among the sons and daughters of God is prepared or qualified to open the book? Who has the mind of God? Who knows the end from the beginning?

The answer comes: "The Lion of the tribe of Juda, the Root of David," even Jesus the Christ (v. 5). He it is who wrought the infinite Atonement, a propitiation that is both timely and timeless, that takes effect before the foundation of the world, thus making it possible for retroactive and proactive redemption to be effected for all the children of God. John sees Jesus, the Lamb "slain from the foundation of the world" (Revelation 13:8; Moses 7:47; see also

v. 6), a Lamb "having twelve horns and twelve eyes, which are the twelve servants of God, sent forth into all the earth" (JST, v. 6), which refers to the Lord and his twelve Apostles.

The Lord Jesus approaches the throne of God and takes the book (see v. 7). The four beasts and the twenty-four elders then fall down before the Lamb and utter a chorus of praise, a new song: "Thou art worthy to take the book, and to open the seals thereof: for thou wast slain, and hast redeemed us to God by thy blood out of every kindred, and tongue, and people, and nation; and hast made us unto our God kings and priests: and we shall reign on the earth" (vv. 8–10). John then watches and listens as the hosts of heaven—"ten thousand times ten thousand, and thousands of thousands" (v. 11)—sing in unison praises to their Messiah: "Worthy is the Lamb that was slain to receive power, and riches, and wisdom, and strength, and honour, and glory, and blessing" (v. 12).

These verses are deeply profound. They make the grand announcement that fallen, mortal men and women, finite and erring souls, may, through accepting the gospel of Jesus Christ by covenant and ordinance, and through spiritual transformation and dedicated discipleship, receive the highest honor and glory and title that one can receive within the holy priesthood of God. Having obtained the fulness of the blessings of the priesthood (which certainly would include the covenants and ordinances of the temple), they become kings and queens, priests and priestesses unto God.[1] As such, they wield the scepter and rule and reign forever.

New Testament scholar N. T. Wright has explained that "humans are not only rescued through Jesus Christ but are *placed in authority over God's new world* [Romans 5:17]. . . .

". . . Jesus Christ has put the human project back on track— actually, more than back on track. It was, all along, God's project *through* human beings *for the whole world*. In Jesus the Messiah,

God has . . . led the human race, at last, to taste the Tree of Life. . . . Humans are called, in and through Jesus Christ, to become what they were always made to be. And what they were made for can be summarized in one single word: glory.

"'Glory' is a standard biblical way of referring to the wise rule of humans over creation. Glory isn't simply a quality that individuals might or might not possess in and for themselves—a splendor, a status, a condition to be admired. Glory is an *active* quality. It is the glorious human rule through which the world is brought to its intended flourishing state, and through which humans themselves come to their own intended flourishing. It is, in fact, 'the glory of God'—the effective rank and status which shows that humans are indeed the God-reflectors, the ones through whom the loving, wise sovereignty of the creator God is brought into powerful, life-giving presence within creation." Finally, Wright observes: "Redeemed humans, then, are to share the 'reign' of Jesus Christ over the new world. But what will be the result of this 'reign'? Nothing short of the renewal of the whole world!"[2]

Revelation 6

The Lamb begins now to open the seals, and John sees a panoramic vision of the history of the world. On rare occasions, John is permitted to see the past. The first seal is opened, revealing the dealings of man during the first thousand years of its temporal existence, or between about 4000 B.C. and 3000 B.C. John sees during this time period a man riding a white horse, "and he that sat on him had a bow; and a crown was given unto him: and he went forth conquering, and to conquer" (v. 2). Who was this great conqueror?

Enoch, the seventh from Adam, was a valiant prophet-leader who might appropriately be termed a conqueror: "And so great was the faith of Enoch that he led the people of God, and their enemies came to battle against them; and he spake the word of the Lord, and the earth trembled. . . ; and all nations feared greatly, so powerful was the word of Enoch, and so great was the power of the language which God had given him. . . . And Enoch continued his preaching in righteousness unto the people of God. And it came to pass in his days, that he built a city that was called the City of Holiness, even Zion. And it came to pass that Enoch talked with the Lord; and he said unto the Lord: Surely Zion shall dwell in safety forever" (Moses 7:13, 19–20).

The opening of the second seal, a revelation of the time period from 3000 B.C. to 2000 B.C., begins with a vision of a man riding a red horse. "And power was given to him that sat thereon to take peace from the earth, and that they should kill one another: and there was given unto him a great sword" (v. 4). This seems to be a clear allusion to the rampant manner in which Satan roamed the earth at this time, particularly during the days of Noah, when filth and wickedness and violence reached pandemic proportions (see Moses 8).

John next witnesses some of the events of the period from 2000 B.C. to 1000 B.C. (third seal), and he observes a man riding a black horse and holding "a pair of balances in his hand" (v. 5). Two different symbolic possibilities might be involved here with balances. First, balances are often used to symbolize scarcity, as in times of famine or economic upheaval. In this sense, the balances may have been symbolic of the great famine in the days of Abraham, a famine so severe that the effects were still being felt in the days of his grandchildren. On the other hand, balances are used to represent justice or law. It was during this same thousand-year period that Jehovah gave the law of Moses to a stumbling and faithless lot of Israelites.

The period of time from 1000 B.C. to the coming of Christ (fourth seal) is seen by John to be a gruesome one. He sees a pale (green) horse, whose rider is named death, "and Hell followed with him. And power was given unto them over the fourth part of the earth, to kill with sword, and with hunger, and with death, and with the beasts of the earth" (v. 8). We know, first of all, that this period was characterized by warfare and bloodshed during the reigns of Saul and David. At the death of Solomon in 975 B.C., the division of the kingdom into Judah and Israel precipitated further hostilities among the Israelites, resulting in death and misery to many. Further, consider the captivities of the house of Israel down to the time of Christ: Assyrian (721 B.C.), Babylonian (558 B.C.), Medo-Persian (538 B.C.), Greek (332 B.C.), and Roman (60 B.C.)

When the Savior opens the fifth seal (Christian era to A.D. 1000), John learns of the Christian martyrs, "the souls of them that were slain for the word of God, and for the testimony which they held" (v. 9). He further sees that these Saints are clothed in "white robes" after suffering death in the flesh (v. 11), for "whoso layeth down his life in my cause, for my name's sake, shall find it again, even life eternal" (D&C 98:13). Joseph Smith is reported to have said about Christian martyrs: "I have, by the aid of the Urim and Thummim . . . , seen those martyrs. They were honest, devoted followers of Christ, according to the light they possessed. They will be saved."[3]

The scenes of the sixth seal (A.D. 1000 to A.D. 2000) are signs of the times, signs incident to the Lord's coming in glory (see vv. 12–17) and of particular interest to us, for John is now witnessing our day. Unusual happenings in the heavens and on the earth are typical of this time; it is a time when the wicked begin to shrink at the thought that the coming of the Son of Man is indeed nigh at hand.

Revelation 7

The events of Revelation 7 are to be accomplished during the sixth thousand years, or after "the opening of the sixth seal" (D&C

77:10). John sees "four angels standing on the four corners of the earth" (v. 1), angels that are "sent forth from God, to whom is given power over the four parts of the earth, to save life and to destroy; these are they who have the everlasting gospel to commit to every nation, kindred, tongue, and people; having power to shut up the heavens, to seal up unto life, or to cast down to the regions of darkness" (D&C 77:8). John then sees another angel (see v. 2), designated in modern revelation as Elias, who has "the seal of the living God over the twelve tribes of Israel; wherefore, he crieth unto the four angels having the everlasting gospel, saying: Hurt not the earth, neither the sea, nor the trees, till we have sealed the servants of our God in their foreheads" (D&C 77:9), meaning sealed men and women unto eternal life and made their calling and election sure.[4]

Joseph Smith taught, "Four destroying angels holding power over the four quarters of the earth until the servants of God are sealed in their foreheads, which signifies sealing the blessing upon their heads, meaning the everlasting covenants, thereby making their calling and election sure. When a seal is put upon the father and mother, it secures their posterity, so that they cannot be lost, but will be saved by virtue of the covenant of their father and mother."[5] Of this statement, Elder Orson F. Whitney noted:

"You parents of the wilful and the wayward. Don't give them up. Don't cast them off. They are not utterly lost. The Shepherd will find his sheep. They were his before they were yours—long before he entrusted them to your care; and you cannot begin to love them as he loves them. They have but strayed in ignorance from the Path of Right, and God is merciful to ignorance. Only the fulness of knowledge brings the fulness of accountability. Our Heavenly Father is far more merciful, infinitely more charitable, than even the best of his servants, and the Everlasting Gospel is mightier in power to save than our narrow finite minds can comprehend.

"The Prophet Joseph Smith declared—and he never taught more comforting doctrine—that the eternal sealings of faithful parents and the divine promises made to them for valiant service in the Cause of Truth, would save not only themselves, but likewise their posterity. Though some of the sheep may wander, the eye of the Shepherd is upon them, and sooner or later they will feel the tentacles of Divine Providence reaching out after them and drawing them back to the fold. Either in this life or in the life to come, they will return. They will have to pay their debt to justice; they will suffer for their sins; and may tread a thorny path; but if it leads them at last, like the penitent Prodigal, to a loving and forgiving father's heart and home, the painful experience will not have been in vain. Pray for your careless and disobedient children; hold on to them with your faith. Hope on, trust on, till you see the salvation of God."[6]

In the same spirit, Elder Boyd K. Packer has provided a comforting context and reaffirmation of the promise to faithful parents. In discussing the "moral pollution" of the last days, he said:

"It is a great challenge to raise a family in the darkening mists of our moral environment.

"We emphasize that the greatest work you will do will be within the walls of your home (see Harold B. Lee, *Ensign*, July 1973, p. 98), and that 'no other success can compensate for failure in the home' (David O. McKay, *Improvement Era*, June 1964, p. 445).

"The measure of our success as parents, however, will not rest solely on how our children turn out. That judgment would be just only if we could raise our families in a perfectly moral environment, and that now is not possible.

"It is not uncommon for responsible parents to lose one of their children, for a time, to influences over which they have no control.

They agonize over rebellious sons or daughters. They are puzzled over why they are so helpless when they have tried so hard to do what they should. It is my conviction that those wicked influences one day will be overruled. . . .

"We cannot overemphasize the value of temple marriage, the binding ties of the sealing ordinance, and the standards of worthiness required of them. When parents keep the covenants they have made at the altar of the temple, their children will be forever bound to them."[7]

John sees 144,000 so sealed, twelve thousand out of all the tribes of Israel, with the exception of Dan (vv. 4–8). The mission of this group of 144,000—"high priests, ordained unto the holy order of God"—will be to "bring as many as will come to the church of the Firstborn" (D&C 77:11). It may be that this number of persons whose charge it is to seal the faithful unto everlasting life is a symbolic expression: in that future day, a day when the restored gospel is found in every nation, kingdom, tongue, and people, a day when temples of the Most High truly dot the earth, men and women all over the world will have matured and developed spiritually to the point that they are qualified for the fulness of temple blessings.

The Revelator then becomes aware of the fact that the Father will save whole hosts of His children. "After this I beheld, and, lo, a great multitude, which no man could number, of all nations, and kindreds, and people, and tongues, stood before the throne, and before the Lamb, clothed with white robes, and palms in their hands; and cried with a loud voice, saying, Salvation to our God which sitteth upon the throne, and unto the Lamb" (vv. 9–10). One of the twenty-four elders asks who such persons are, and the Savior responds, "These are they which came out of great tribulation, and have washed their robes, and made them white in the blood of the Lamb" (vv. 13–14).

Revelation 8:1–5

The opening of the seventh seal (A.D. 2000 to the end of the Millennium) reveals a strange phenomenon: "silence in heaven about the space of half an hour" (v. 1; see also D&C 88:95). The strangeness of this event lies in the fact that the heavens and the earth had been the scene of unusual happenings since the opening of the *sixth* seal. Whether the period of half an hour is according to our time (thirty minutes) or according to the reckoning of God's time (where one Kolob day equals a thousand earth years and half an hour equals approximately twenty-one years), we do not know. This may well refer to great wickedness in the last days—evil and pollution that seal the heavens to the ungodly. In our dispensation the Lord has declared, "For *all flesh is corrupted* before me; and *the powers of darkness prevail* upon the earth, among the children of men, in the presence of all the hosts of heaven—*which causeth silence to reign,* and all eternity is pained" (D&C 38:11–12; emphasis added).

Seven angels, each with a trumpet, are then shown to John (see v. 2). We are given to understand that "the sounding of the trumpets of the seven angels are the preparing and finishing of [the Lord's] work, in the beginning of the seventh thousand years—the preparing of the way before the time of his coming" (D&C 77:12). These seven angels begin now to unleash the chaos and destruction incident to the Lord's coming, a running account of which continues from Revelation 8:6 through 11:19.

5

THE SEVEN TRUMPETS (8:6–11:19)

Revelation 8:6–13

In Revelation 8, four of the seven angels sound their trumpets (or issue judgments), which are as follows:

First angel: Hail, fire, and blood are sent to earth, killing all green grass, and a third part of all trees (see v. 7).

Second angel: A great mountain, burning with fire, is cast into the sea, turning a third part of the sea to blood (see Jeremiah 51:25; Amos 7:4). This brings death to a third of all marine life and destruction to a third of all ships on the sea (see vv. 8–9).

Third angel: A great star, burning like a giant lamp, falls from heaven and strikes the earth, defiling the waters and bringing death to many (vv. 10–11). Could John be witnessing the results of atomic fallout?[1] John calls the star and the third part of the waters "Wormwood" (v. 11), perhaps applying the words of Jeremiah, who warned that God will give to his people wormwood and gall to drink because of their idolatry (see Jeremiah 9:15; 23:15). Wormwood is bitter, and some species are poisonous.

Fourth angel: The sun, moon, and stars are "smitten," so that one third of the light of both day and night is taken away (v. 12).

At this point the sounding of the angels' trumpets is interrupted by an *eagle* (not an angel)[2] "flying through the midst of heaven, saying with a loud voice, Woe, woe, woe, to the inhabiters

32

of the earth by reason of the other voices of the trumpet of the three angels, which are yet to sound!" (v. 13).

Revelation 9

We are reminded in modern revelation that the events found in Revelation 9 "are to be accomplished after the opening of the seventh seal, before the coming of Christ" (D&C 77:13). The fifth angel sounds his trumpet, and John sees Lucifer, "a star" (v. 1; see also Revelation 12:1–17), open the bottomless pits of hell and release upon the earth every evil influence conceivable. Out of the (figurative) smoke of the great furnace of perdition come myriad "locusts" (v. 3), no doubt wicked persons, having almost unlimited power to torment and torture mankind.[3] They are commanded "that they should not hurt the grass of the earth, neither any green thing, neither any tree" but rather those on the earth who have not received the assurance of eternal life through receiving the mark of God on their foreheads (v. 4). True safety in that day will come only through being among the pure in heart in Zion, which will be "a land of peace, a city of refuge, a place of safety for the saints of the Most High God; and the glory of the Lord shall be there, and the terror of the Lord also shall be there, insomuch that the wicked will not come unto it, and it shall be called Zion" (D&C 45:66–67). The locusts are given power to cause great suffering to the remainder of the people on the earth, a torment so hideous that "in those days shall men seek death, and shall not find it" (v. 6).

John now attempts to describe types of warfare with which he is totally unfamiliar, and like Isaiah and Joel, he speaks in as clear a language as he can of things foreign to his experience, of a time when weapons and methods of warfare are most terrible (see vv. 7–10, 17–19). This group of demons is not leaderless; they have a king over them, Satan—called "the angel of the bottomless pit" by John, called *Abaddon* in Hebrew and *Apollyon* in Greek (v. 11).

The sixth angel sounds his trumpet, and John is permitted to see hosts of "horsemen," 200 million in number, issuing death to the ungodly of the earth. The morbid vision reveals that one-third of all inhabitants on the earth are destroyed by the mighty horsemen (vv. 16–18). We will speak of the battle of Armageddon shortly.

Revelation 10

An angel next appears in great glory, holding in his hand a little book. The angel cries out with a loud voice, followed by the sounding of seven thunders uttering their voice. The message of the seven thunders must have been highly significant, for John hastens to write what he has just heard. Suddenly a voice from heaven explains that those things are sealed up "which the seven thunders uttered"; therefore, "write them not" (v. 4). This would seem to be detailed information concerning the signs of the times and the end of the world that is not yet to be made known to mortals.[4]

The same voice from heaven now instructs John to "go and take the little book" from the angel. The glorious angel gives the book, which is open, to John and says to him, "Take it, and eat it up; and it shall make thy belly bitter, but it shall be in thy mouth sweet as honey" (v. 9). The eating of the little book represents "a mission, and *an ordinance* [requiring appropriate priesthood keys received from Moses on the Mount of Transfiguration (Matthew 16:19; 17:1–3; D&C 110:11)[5]], for him to gather the tribes of Israel" (D&C 77:14; emphasis added). The gathering of the chosen people in the latter days, though difficult and challenging (bitter), would prove to be deeply rewarding and joyous (sweet). Finally the angel told John that he must prophesy before many nations and kings and tongues and people (see v. 11). As a translated being, John has been made as "flaming fire and a ministering angel; he shall minister for those who shall be heirs of salvation who dwell on the earth" (D&C 7:6).

Revelation 11

The scene seems to change somewhat as John is commanded, "Rise, and measure the temple of God" (v. 1)—he is to study the condition of the Church and assess the strengths and weaknesses of its members. Verse 2 then indicates that John sees the overthrow of the holy city (Jerusalem) by the Gentiles and the night of universal apostasy that follows.

We move forward in time now. John sees two witnesses, "two prophets that are to be raised up to the Jewish nation in the last days" (D&C 77:15), who preach and prophesy for three and a half years (see v. 3). These two prophesy to the Jews in Jerusalem in sackcloth and attire indicative of mourning; they are no doubt predicting doom. The fact that John refers to them as "the two olive trees, and the two candlesticks" (v. 4; oil is used to light the lamps of faith, while lamp stands light the path for all who truly seek God); and the fact that they have power to call down fire from heaven like Elijah of old, and power to shut the heavens, cause drought, and "smite the earth" with pestilence like Nephi the son of Helaman (vv. 5–6; see 1 Kings 17–18; Helaman 10:6–7) seems to point to the conclusion that they are legal administrators possessed of the power of God, the keys of the kingdom, "*members of the Council of the Twelve or of the First Presidency of the Church.*"[6]

As with testators of ages past, when their witness is borne and their mission is ended, "the beast that ascendeth out of the bottomless pit," wicked men, pawns in the hands of Satan, "shall overcome them, and kill them" (v. 7). Their dead bodies will lie unburied in the streets of Jerusalem for three and a half days, while the ungodly rejoice over their murderous actions and the fact that these two gospel gadflies, these conscience-pricking witnesses, will trouble them no more. At the end of the three and a half days, these prophets will be resurrected and ascend into heaven amidst the malevolent multitudes, and great fear will come upon all who behold (vv. 8–13).

The consummation of the two prophets' work would seem to take place just prior to the coming of the Savior to the Mount of Olives to deliver the Jews from destruction, at the end of the battle of Armageddon. This may be inferred from the fact that following the resurrection of the two witnesses, John's account states that at "the same hour was there a great earthquake, and the tenth part of the city fell, and in the earthquake were slain of men seven thousand: and the remnant were affrighted, and gave glory to the God of heaven" (v. 13).[7]

John then watches as the seventh angel sounds his trumpet, and great voices in heaven declare that the age of Satanic triumph is finished and he whose right it is to reign will now reign forever: "The kingdoms of this world are become the kingdoms of our Lord, and of his Christ; and he shall reign for ever and ever" (v. 15; see also Daniel 2:44).

6

THE SEVEN SIGNIFICANT
SIGNS (12:1–14:20)

Revelation 12

Revelation 12 received particular attention from Joseph Smith as he undertook his inspired translation of the King James Version of the Bible: the Prophet changed 95 percent of the verses. First, in verse 1, John sees a great sign in heaven, "in the likeness of things on the earth" (JST, Revelation 12:1). A woman, representing the Church of God in the meridian dispensation, is seen by John (JST, Revelation 12:7). She is "clothed with the sun" (v. 1), which is descriptive of the Church of the Lamb in all its glory, power, and perfection, a church which works to prepare its members for the glory of the sun (Son). This woman also has "the moon under her feet" (v. 1), indicating that the churches of the world (terrestrial ones— like unto the moon) are lower in glory or beneath the true church of the Lamb. Upon the head of the woman, or church of God, is a crown of twelve stars, depicting, undoubtedly, the twelve Apostles of the Lamb, placed at the head of the Church.

John beholds that the woman brings forth a man-child, "who was to rule all nations with a rod of iron" (v. 5) or iron rod—the word of God (see 1 Nephi 11:25). This man-child was the political kingdom of God, which could have been established in the meridian of time and could have helped to usher in millennial government. It is called "the kingdom of our God and his Christ" (JST,

Revelation 12:7). The power of the adversary is great, however, and the political program of the kingdom in its fulness is not put in place. Hence John speaks of the child being "caught up unto God, and to his throne" (v. 5). President John Taylor taught the important principle here under consideration—that the Church of God (spiritual) gives birth to the larger kingdom of God (political):

"We talk sometimes about the Church of God, and why? We talk about the kingdom of God, and why? Because, before there could be a kingdom of God, there must be a Church of God, and hence the first principles of the Gospel were needed to be preached to all nations, as they were formerly when the Lord Jesus Christ and others made their appearance on the earth. And why so? Because of the impossibility of introducing the law of God among a people who would not be subject to and guided by the spirit of revelation."[1]

A "great red dragon, having seven heads and ten horns, and seven crowns upon his heads" (v. 3), probably representing the Roman Empire (see details in Revelation 13), wages war against the woman and, after much persecution, drives the woman into the wilderness, or the Church into a state of apostasy (see also D&C 86:3). The Lord removes his Church from the earth speedily, or as John stated, "to the woman were given two wings of a great eagle, that she might fly into the wilderness" (v. 14). There she is to remain 1,260 years or, stated another way, "a time [360 years], and times [360 x 2 = 720 years], and half a time [180 years]" (v. 14; see also JST, Revelation 12:5). Satan hates the Church and continues to wage war against "the remnant of her seed" (v. 17), the latter-day Church restored through Joseph Smith.

What is the origin of evil in the world? John answers this question through an interpolative group of verses in the middle of Revelation 12. The war between good and evil began in the premortal existence in what we know as the War in Heaven. John teaches, "And there was war in heaven; Michael and his angels fought against the dragon; and the dragon and his angels fought against Michael" (JST, Revelation 12:6).

Next, John ties that first battle against evil with the battle waged in the meridian of time with this statement: "And the dragon prevailed not against Michael, *neither the child,* nor the woman which was the church of God, who had been delivered of her pains, and *brought forth the kingdom of our God and his Christ*" (JST, Revelation 12:7; emphasis added). We learn in modern revelation that the devil rebelled against God, saying, "Give me thine honor, which is my power; and also a third part of the hosts of heaven turned he away from me because of [their improper exercise of] their agency; and they were thrust down, and thus came the devil and his angels; and, behold, there is a place prepared for them from the beginning, which place is hell" (D&C 29:36–38; see also 76:25–30; Moses 4:1–4; Abraham 3:27–28).

The Prophet Joseph stated: "The contention in heaven was— Jesus said there would be certain souls that would not be saved; and the devil said he could save them all, and laid his plans before the grand council, who gave their vote in favor of Jesus Christ. So the devil rose up in rebellion against God, and was cast down, with all who put up their heads for him."[2] Indeed, as John attests, the armies of Michael overcame Lucifer and his hosts "by the blood of the Lamb, and by the word of their testimony; for they loved not their own lives, but kept the testimony even unto death" (JST, v. 11).

Revelation 13

We come now to a part of the vision of John that has caused perhaps more discussion and speculation than any other section. The Lord has revealed little concerning the details of Revelation 13, and so we turn to those few things we do know about John, his day, the enemies of the Church, and the people to whom he wrote, in hopes that we might discern at least the major message.

The difficult section begins, "And I saw another sign, *in the likeness of the kingdoms of the earth;* a beast rise up out of the sea, and he stood upon the sand of the sea, having seven heads and ten horns; and upon his horns ten crowns; and upon his heads the name of blasphemy" (JST, Revelation 13:1; emphasis added). In this case (as contrasted with Revelation 4, where John sees literal beasts in heaven), the Revelator now sees an *image* of a beast, or a *figure* of a beast, representative of "those kingdoms which had degenerated and become corrupt, savage and beast-like in their dispositions, even the degenerate kingdoms of the wicked world."[3] But what of the specifics of this beast?

Perhaps the most fearsome beast John could behold was the Roman Empire with its heathen practices and emperor worship. Now, what of the heads, horns, and crowns? From the time of Octavius (Augustus) Caesar until the days of John the Beloved's Apocalypse, the Roman Empire had the following men at its head:

Augustus: 27 B.C.–A.D. 14
Tiberius: A.D. 14–A.D. 37
Caligula: A.D. 37–A.D. 41
Claudius: A.D. 41–A.D. 54
Nero: A.D. 54–A.D. 68
Galba, Otho, Vitellius (three military generals who
     acted as leaders of Rome for about eighteen months):
     A.D. June 68–December 69
Vespasian: A.D. 69–A.D. 79
Titus: A.D. 79–A.D. 81
Domitian: A.D. 81–A.D. 96

To attempt an interpretation of Revelation 13, we will pay particular attention to two of these emperors, Nero and Domitian.

Nero Caesar began the first persecutions of the Christians by the Roman government. His entire life was one of whim, pleasure, and waste, and it ended, as do the lives of so many of those who finally exploit and exhaust the senses, in suicide. The evilness with which Nero was viewed may well be appreciated by the fact that many people seriously wondered if he had really died. Others became convinced that *if* he were dead, he would surely return with even greater power and added cruelty. This latter idea has become known in Christian history as the Nero *redivivus* myth. As strange as it may seem, John may have even employed this popular myth in his writing of Revelation.

Domitian was even more base and cruel than Nero. He, like Nero, became obsessed with his own personal divinity, but he carried things one step further by insisting that he be worshipped as a god. Many persons began to recognize similarities between the two evil emperors, and some concluded that Domitian was actually not the eighth major Roman head but the seventh, since in reality he was the reincarnated Nero.

The seven heads might then consist of the seven major Roman emperors, Augustus through Titus, except Domitian, who "was, and is not, even he is the eighth, and *is of the seven*" (Revelation 17:11; emphasis added). The ten horns and ten crowns would therefore be the total number of Roman leaders, minus Domitian, during the 108-year period.

John sees the beast, or the Roman Empire, receive its power and authority from the dragon, or Satan (see v. 2). Next he writes, "And I saw one of his heads as it were wounded to death; and his deadly wound was healed" (v. 3). This would seem to be a clear allusion to the death and subsequent return of Nero. Following this, "all the world [wonders] after the beast" (v. 3) or seems to be held in awe by the strange possibility that Nero would return to earth.

The Revelator then beholds the people of the earth

worshipping Satan as well as the Roman Empire. Extolling the virtues and powers of the empire, they cry out in unison, "Who is like unto the beast? who is able to make war with him?" (v. 4). The beast makes war with the Saints, overcomes them, and gains power over all nations and people (see v. 7).

Another beast comes up out of the earth, one having "two horns like a lamb, and [yet] he spake as a dragon" (v. 11). This beast may well be an anti-Christ, a mirror image of Christ, since he *appears like* a Lamb (see also Matthew 24:5, 24) but speaks like the devil. He exercises the same power as the first beast (Roman Empire), and he causes all people "to worship the first beast" (v. 12). We next learn that all miraculous events are not inspired of God: John views the anti-Christ as he performs great wonders, all of which deceive the people of the day (see vv. 13–14).

Just as the God of heaven places a mark (seal) upon those whom he claims as his, even so do the god of this world (Satan) and his anti-Christs cause all who are in league with them to receive the mark of the beast, "a mark in their right hand, or in their foreheads: And . . . no man might buy or sell, save he that had the mark, or the name of the beast, or the number of his name" (vv. 16–17). Then comes verse 18, one of the strangest and yet most popular verses in Revelation: "Here is wisdom. Let him that hath understanding count the number of the beast: for *it is the number of a man*; and his number is Six hundred threescore and six" (emphasis added).

John tells us that the mark of the beast is "the name of the beast, or the number of his name" (v. 17). Many have used spurious reasoning to conclude that the number 666 was somehow associated with Adolf Hitler, the Roman Catholic pope, IBM, or a whole host of candidates, but a more careful consideration reveals its reference to the emperor Nero.

By translating the Greek Νέρων Καίσαρ (Neron Caesar) into

Hebrew letters and giving them their numerical equivalents (the Hebrew and Greek languages use the letters of the alphabet as numbers), we get the following: (200) ר + (60) ס + (100) ק + (50) ן + (6) ו + (200) ר + (50) נ. The total is 666.[4]

This interpretation of Revelation 13:17–18 is one option among many but perhaps the most fascinating. It is not, however, without its critics. New Testament scholar Leon Morris explained:

"In modern times the most favored solution is 'Nero Caesar' (if the final letter be omitted to give the equivalent of the Latin spelling of the name the total is 666). But to get this result we must use the Greek form of the Latin name, transliterated into Hebrew characters, and with a variant spelling at that. . . . This solution has its attractions, but no one has shown why a Hebrew name with an unusual spelling should be employed in a Greek writing. It is also to be borne in mind that in the ancient world when Nero was a considerable figure (the Nero *redivivus* myth is thought by many critics to underlie parts of Revelation), this solution was apparently never thought of. . . .

"Other solutions are put forward, but none has won wide acceptance. It is possible that such solutions are on the wrong lines and that we should understand the expression purely in terms of the symbolism of numbers. If we take the sum of the values represented by the letters of the name *Iēsous*, the Greek name 'Jesus,' it comes to 888; each digit is one more than seven, the perfect number. But 666 yields the opposite phenomenon, for each digit falls short. The number may be meant to indicate not an individual, but a persistent falling short. All the more is this likely to be correct if we translate 'it is the number of man' rather than 'a man.' John will then be saying that unregenerate man is persistently evil. He bears the mark of the beast in all he does. Civilization without Christ is necessarily under the dominion of the evil one."[5]

We must never forget that the primary purpose of the

Revelation of John the Apostle was to reveal "things which must be hereafter" (4:1) and which therefore dealt with futurity. It seems appropriate, after discussing possible meanings of Revelation 13, to point out that John may well have been writing about two (or more) periods of history: his day (and immediately following it) and an age far in the future, a time just preceding the coming of the Lord in glory. Surely John's prophecies, like those given by many of his prophetic associates, could have and will have dual (or multiple) fulfillment.

Revelation 14

The next thing to enter John's visual field is the Savior standing upon Mount Zion in Independence, Missouri, and with the Master, the 144,000 special high priests who have the seal of eternal life upon their heads and the sealing power within their grasp (see v. 1). In the revelation we know as the appendix of the Doctrine and Covenants, we learn that "the hour of his coming is nigh—when the Lamb shall stand upon Mount Zion, and with him a hundred and forty-four thousand, having his Father's name written on their foreheads" (D&C 133:17–18). Elder Orson Pratt observed: "They, the one hundred and forty-four thousand, had a peculiar inscription in their foreheads. What was it? It was the Father's name. What is the Father's name? It is God—the being we worship. If, then, the one hundred and forty-four thousand are to have the name of God inscribed on their foreheads, will it be . . . something that has no meaning? or will it mean that which the inscriptions specify?—that they are indeed Gods—one with the Father and one with the Son."[6]

John then listens as this great body of high priests sing "a new song before the throne" of God (v. 3), "a song of victory and triumph; a song hailing Christ's Millennial reign, a song proclaiming that the kingdoms of this world are swept away, and that the true King of Earth now dwells with men; a song of redemption and glory and honor; a song that cannot be sung until the promised day of peace and righteousness arrives."[7] This group of 144,000 are virgins, meaning they are untainted by the ways of the world, pure-hearted, guileless, true, and faithful disciples (vv. 4–5).

At this point John sees "another angel fly in the midst of heaven, having the everlasting gospel to preach unto them that dwell on the earth" (v. 6). Yes, this is Moroni as well as every heavenly visitor with a message or authority, every Elias, a *composite angel*, who came to restore the ancient order of things. It is Moroni, Michael, Peter, James, John, John the Baptist, Gabriel, Raphael, Moses, Elias, Elijah, and all others with important keys and instructions reserved for the dispensation of the fulness of times.[8]

Another angel appears, saying that the great city of wickedness, Babylon, Satan's countereffort to God's Zion, "is fallen," even she who made all men to drink "the wine of the wrath of God," the consequence of her fornication with the things of the world (vv. 8–10). Another "voice from heaven" (v. 13) sounds the comforting assurance that blessed is the state of those who die "in the Lord," for such will not taste the bitterness of death (which is sin), but death to such will be a sweet transitional experience (see D&C 42:46).

John then witnesses (see vv. 14–16) the fulfillment of that great prophetic parable, the wheat and the tares (see Matthew 13:24–30; D&C 86:1–7), in which the Son of Man, leading the reaping angels, prepares to thrust in the sickle that separates and destroys. Another angel is sent to administer destruction; his task is to gather "the vine of the earth [the earth is ripe in iniquity], and cast it into the great winepress of the wrath of God" (v. 19).

7

THE SEVEN LAST PLAGUES (15:1–16:21)

Revelation 15

Revelation 15 opens with another glimpse of the "sea of glass mingled with fire" (v. 2), the abode of the righteous, the earth in its sanctified and immortal state (see D&C 77:1; 130:7, 9). In this atmosphere of the "everlasting burnings" of God (Isaiah 33:14; see also D&C 137:1–3), the exalted continue a song of praise to the Almighty. But John's attention is called back from the joys of celestial glory to the realities of the carnage awaiting the wicked before the coming of Christ. One of the four beasts spoken of earlier (Revelation 4) gives unto "seven angels seven golden vials full of the wrath of God" (v. 7). These are the seven last plagues to be sent upon the wicked, "full of the wrath of God, who liveth for ever and ever" (v. 7).

Revelation 16

A voice is heard from the heavens (see v. 1), and the seven angels, with their seven vials of wrath, enter upon their final mission of destruction. The seven last plagues are then spoken of as follows:

First plague: A "noisome [bad, evil] and grievous sore," perhaps like ulcers, upon all who have the mark of the beast or have worshipped the image of the beast (v. 2; see Revelation 13). Zechariah declared, "Their flesh shall consume away while they stand upon their feet, and their eyes shall consume away in their holes, and their tongue shall consume away in their mouth" (Zechariah 14:12; see also D&C 29:19; Exodus 9:8–12).

Second plague: The second vial (see v. 3) is poured out upon the sea, turning the sea to blood and bringing death to everything living in the sea (see also Exodus 7:14–25). Note the following from modern revelation: "Behold, I, the Lord, in the beginning blessed the waters; but in the last days, by the mouth of my servant John, I cursed the waters. Wherefore, the days will come that no flesh shall be safe upon the waters" (D&C 61:14–15). Compare this with the second trumpet judgment sent in Revelation 8:8.

Third plague: The third angel (see vv. 4–6) empties his vial upon the rivers and springs, causing them to be changed to blood (see also Exodus 7:19). This third angel then expresses his pleasure and delight in the justice of the Almighty, who causes those who shed the innocent blood of the Saints to now drink blood. Compare this vial with the fourth trumpet judgment sent in Revelation 8.

Fourth plague: The sun is changed so that it burns the wicked "with great heat" (v. 9). Perhaps, like Elijah, the fourth angel is able to hold the sun in its path until it selectively tortures the wicked. Compare this vial with the fourth trumpet judgment sent in Revelation 8.

Fifth plague: The fifth plague (see vv. 10–11) is a direct assault on the throne of the devil. Darkness covers the kingdom of the evil one, symbolizing (1) the spread of spiritual darkness among the ungodly or (2) the gradual waning of the power of Satan and his forces (see also Exodus 10:4–15, 21–29).

Sixth plague: The waters of the River Euphrates dry up, "that the way of the kings of the east might be prepared" (v. 12). This is not further explained, but "in the Old Testament a mighty action of God is frequently associated with the drying up of waters, as the Red Sea (Ex. 14:21), the Jordan (Jos. 3:16–17), and several times in prophecy (Is. 11:15; Je. 51:36; Zc. 10:11). Beyond the Roman Empire, east of Euphrates, was for John's readers 'a great unknown land.' Who could tell what mighty kings lurked there? The Parthians lived in that area and during the first century there was a persistent fear that they would invade the Empire. This was reinforced by the Nero *redivivus* myth, which affirmed that Nero would put himself at the head of the Parthian hordes and march into the Empire.

"John is suggesting that at the End all these fears and more will be realized. We should bear in mind that Nero and his armies in the myth were not going to ally themselves with Rome, but to attack her. So John is thinking of division among the forces of evil (see 17:16), not of a united front. But we would be wrong in holding that he is doing no more than voice a contemporary expectation. By appealing to contemporary fears he is making the point that at the end of time the divided forces of evil (cf. 17:16) will engage in a terrible conflict. Curiously, having told us that the way will be cleared for the mighty potentates to march westward, John does not follow this up. He does not say that the kings used the way prepared for them. In fact he does not mention them again."[1]

John then sees all of the nations gathered together to fight against the Jews in the valley of Armageddon (see also Ezekiel 38:16–39; Zechariah 14:2). Of Armageddon, Elder Bruce R. McConkie has written: "The kings of the earth and of the whole world will gather to fight the battle of that great day of God Almighty. Their command center will be at Armageddon, overlooking the valley of Megiddo. All nations will be gathered against Jerusalem. Two hundred thousand thousand warriors and more— two hundred million men of arms and more—shall come forth to conquer or die on the plains of Esdraelon and in all the nations of the earth. At the height of this war, the Lord Jesus will put his foot on the Mount of Olives and save his ancient covenant people." In short, "This, in truth, will be a worldwide conflict; the sword that is wielded in the mountains of Israel will be the same sword that slays men in all nations."[2]

Seventh plague: The seventh angel pours "his vial into the air" (vv. 17–21), and there follows cataclysmic occurrences. Thunders, lightnings, and the massive earthquake caused by the Savior's descent to the Mount of Olives (Revelation 11) then follow. Not only is the great city of Jerusalem divided into three parts but also "the islands shall become one land; and the land of Jerusalem and the land of Zion [Independence, Missouri] shall be turned back into their own place, and the earth shall be like as it was in the days before it was divided" (D&C 133:23–24). John also notices that there falls upon the wicked huge hailstones, each stone weighing a talent—anywhere from forty-five to one hundred pounds, depending on the system of weights and measures used! But as is the case so many times before in John's revelation, the wicked refuse to repent but rather continue to blaspheme the name of God.

8

THE TRIUMPH OF ALMIGHTY GOD (17:1–20:15)

Revelation 17

The effects of the seventh angel's vial continue to be felt, as John records in Revelation 17 and 18 the fall of the great and abominable church, every church and organization (social, economic, political, fraternal, or religious) that is not allied with the Church of the Lamb of God or that fights against the establishment of the kingdom of God (see 2 Nephi 10:16). One of the seven angels (which one we are not told) beckons John to come forward and view "the judgment of the great whore that sitteth upon many waters" (v. 1), that has had a degrading effect upon "peoples, and multitudes, and nations, and tongues" (v. 15). John is told that the great whore is one "with whom the kings of the earth have committed fornication, and the inhabitants of the earth have been made drunk with the wine of her fornication" (v. 2).

"To a greater or lesser degree, as the case may be, all of the governments of the earth are in league with the great whore in that, from time to time, they do such things as the following:

"Prohibit the worship of God;

"Enact laws defining religious beliefs and prescribing forms of worship;

"Maintain state-supported, false systems of religion;

"Deny freedom of religious belief to all their citizens;

"Impose the religious beliefs of conquerors upon conquered people;

"Permit the mingling of religious influence with civil government;

"Foster one religious society and proscribe another;

"Deny to men their inherent and inalienable rights;

"Fail to guarantee the free exercise of conscience, the right and control of property, and the protection of life;

"Enact laws which curtail the agency of man;

"Require the teaching of false principles in their educational systems;

"Deny the representatives of certain churches the right to teach their doctrines or proselyte among their people; and

"Fail to punish crime and protect the rights of their citizens, particularly unpopular minority groups."[1]

The Revelator sees a woman sitting "upon a scarlet coloured beast, full of names of blasphemy, having seven heads and ten horns" (v. 3). This statement links (from a contemporary first century point of view) the harlot with the Roman Empire, especially when we (1) read in verse 9 that the seven heads represent seven mountains (Rome is a city founded on seven hills) and (2) when we consider that the last verse of the chapter (v. 18) states simply that the woman "is that great city, which reigneth over the kings of the earth." Even more specifically, many scholars feel that the woman is Roma, the goddess of Rome.

Let us now attempt to give some meaning to the difficult verses 10 and 11. If we apply the Nero *redivivus* myth (chapter 13), one approach might be: "And there are seven kings [the seven major Roman emperors from Augustus through Titus; remember, Domitian was considered by some to be Nero again]: five are fallen [Augustus through Nero had died], and one is [Vespasian], and the other is not yet come; and when he cometh, he must continue a short space. [Titus, next in line, only reigned for two years.] And the beast that was, and is not [Nero], even he is the eighth, and is of the seven, and goeth into perdition."

This approach to the interpretation works fairly well as long as we do not press the issue that the book of Revelation was believed to have been written during the reign of Domitian (A.D. 81–96) and not during the time of Vespasian (A.D. 69–79). There are those, however, who believe that the Revelation was written soon after A.D. 70. If this is the case, we might feel more comfortable with the preceding explanation.

Another explanation, somewhat different, is that the kings in verse 10 symbolize not individual rulers but *empires*. The five that are fallen are the Old Babylonian, the Assyrian, the New Babylonian, the Medo-Persian, and the Graeco-Macedonian. The one that is the Roman, the seventh yet future, may stand for "'all anti-christian governments between the fall of Rome and the final empire of antichrist.' Since the eighth is 'of the seven,' the final kingdom of antichrist may well arise in one of the ancient seats of empire."[2]

We must remember that John is also writing concerning the fall of the church of the devil in the last days. The day is yet future when the kings of the earth will come to hate the whore of the earth; after much dissension they will overcome her and be instruments in the hands of the Lord (ironically) in bringing about her total downfall. An excellent description and scriptural commentary on the nature and fall of the great and abominable church is found in the Book of Mormon (1 Nephi 13–14, 22).

Revelation 18

Revelation 18 continues the vision of the fall of spiritual Babylon. John sees a glorious angel come down and cry "mightily with a strong voice, saying, Babylon the great is fallen, is fallen"

(v. 2). Another voice from the heavens appeals to the people of God to come out of the influence and grips of the dying whore (see v. 4): "Go ye out from among the nations, even from Babylon, from the midst of wickedness, which is spiritual Babylon" (D&C 133:14).

John notices that the kings of the earth (especially those who have committed fornication with her against the true God) mourn and lament for the mother of harlots, as do the merchants of the earth, who, with her, profited at the expense of the ignorant (see vv. 9–19). Wicked and worldly businessmen who, with the great and abominable church, did buy and sell gold and silver, "fine-twined linen, and the precious clothing" (1 Nephi 13:8) and who did bargain over the souls of men will now lament the destruction of their companion in corruption. The role of the great harlot in persecuting the Church of God is then clarified in the closing statement by John: "And in her was found the blood of prophets, and of saints, and of all that were slain upon the earth" (v. 24).

Revelation 19

The Apostle now hears many voices in heaven singing praises unto the Lord and declaring his judgments against the great whore to be just and true (vv. 1–6). The praises and rejoicing continue as the hosts of heaven realize that the marriage and marriage supper of the Lamb are imminent (vv. 7–9). Christ (the Bridegroom) will come to his Bride (the Church), and a great wedding (the Second Coming) will reward the faithful. "And to her [the bride] was granted that she should be arrayed in fine linen, clean and white: for the fine linen is the righteousness of saints" (v. 8; see also Matthew 22:1–4 and JST, Luke 14:16–24 for the Savior's teachings in the parable of the wedding feast).

The heavens open and John sees the Savior, "called Faithful and True," riding on a white horse. Christ's "eyes were as a flame of fire, and on his head were many crowns; and he had a name written, that no man knew, but he himself" (vv. 11–12). The armies in heaven, clothed in pure and white linen, also ride white horses and join Jesus at this point. The inscription on the clothing of the Redeemer-General is a glorious one: King of Kings and Lord of Lords. This mighty army goes to battle against the kings and armies of the world to finally establish in the minds of every soul that Jesus Christ reigns forever (see vv. 14–16).

The armies of the Lord then take the beast, Satan and his co-workers (the anti-Christs, the false prophets, and all that have received the mark of the beast or that worshipped the image of the beast), and cast them into hell (see vv. 19–20), where "their torment is as a lake of fire and brimstone" (2 Nephi 9:16). At the coming of Christ, the wicked will be burned because of their inability to abide the glory of the Messiah. Their spirits will then go into the spirit world and take up residence in hell, to suffer and repent and wait, while those of terrestrial and celestial natures will live on the transformed millennial earth.

Revelation 20

We learn that the Millennium will be a marvelous time in which to live. John watches as Satan is bound for a thousand years so that he may tempt and deceive men no more (see vv. 1–2). The Millennium is brought in by power and maintained by the righteousness of earth's inhabitants (see 1 Nephi 22:26). The "end of the world is in fact the destruction of the wicked" at the time of Christ's coming in glory (see Joseph Smith–Matthew 1:4, 31).[3] The angel "cast him [Satan] into the bottomless pit, and shut him up, and set a seal upon him, that he should deceive the nations no more, till the thousand years should be fulfilled: and after that he must be loosed a little season" (v. 3). "And again, verily, verily, I say unto you that when the thousand years are ended, and men again begin to deny their God, then will I spare the earth but for a little season" (D&C 29:22).

But why would people living on a paradisiacal, terrestrial, Edenic earth begin to deny God? Why would anyone turn away from the glorious light of millennial splendor, treat lightly the spirit of grace, and deny God? If we take the Book of Mormon as a pattern, we note that following the time of the risen Lord's ministry among his American Hebrews, the people enjoyed a mini-Millennium, a period of almost two hundred years of conversion to Christ, full and complete consecration, universal prosperity, and love and devotion to one another (see 4 Nephi 1:2–3). But then, in the 201st year following the birth of the Savior, pride once again raised its ugly head, such that people became more concerned with what they were called, how they looked, and how much they possessed. And then come these haunting words: "And from that time forth they did have their goods and their substance no more common among them" (4 Nephi 1:25). Similarly, President George Q. Cannon taught that at the end of the Millennium, pride will again afflict earth's inhabitants and will cause them to be consumed with their own wants rather than the needs of their fellows. They will reject the law of consecration, lose the Spirit, and deny and defy.[4]

John sees individual kingdoms established, each man presiding over his posterity. He sees the martyrs for the cause of Christ. These all "lived and reigned with Christ a thousand years" (v. 4). Joseph Smith clarified this point—the reign of Christ on earth—when he said: "Christ and the resurrected Saints will reign over the earth during the thousand years. They will not probably dwell upon the earth, but will visit it when they please, or when it is necessary to govern it."[5]

John continues his account: "But the rest of the dead [telestial] lived not again [on the earth] until the thousand years were finished. This is [the blessing of] the first resurrection. Blessed and

holy is he that hath part in the first resurrection: on such the second death [second spiritual death, final separation of man from
God] hath no power, but they shall be priests of God and of Christ,
and shall reign with him a thousand years" (vv. 5–6). In describing
those who inherit the celestial kingdom, the revelation states:
"They are they who are the church of the Firstborn. They are they
into whose hands the Father has given all things—they are
they who are priests and kings, who have received of his fulness,
and of his glory; and are priests of the Most High, after the order of
Melchizedek, which was after the order of Enoch, which was after
the order of the Only Begotten Son" (D&C 76:54–57). Truly, "all
those who are ordained unto this priesthood are made like unto
the Son of God, abiding a priest continually" (JST, Hebrews 7:3).

John's feelings of peace and bliss from viewing the paradisiacal earth are interrupted as he views the scenes that lie ahead (see
vv. 7–8). The devil is loosed from his prison "for a little season"
at the end of the Millennium, "that he may gather together his
armies" (D&C 88:111). John watches as Satan stalks the earth
once again, going among the nations, Gog and Magog (representing all the hosts of the wicked), and gathering his forces, which,
sadly enough, number "as the sand of the sea" (v. 8). Joseph Smith
declared simply, "The battle of Gog and Magog will be after the
millennium."[6] Following this final battle between good and evil,
Satan and his disciples are cast forever into outer darkness. This
period of time, that day when the earth is cleansed by fire a second
time and readied for celestial glory, is called in scripture "the end of
the earth" (D&C 38:5; 43:31; 88:101; Joseph Smith–Matthew 1:55).

Now comes a vision of the last resurrection (see vv. 12–15), the
raising of those who are telestial or who are the sons of perdition;
this occurs at the end of the Millennium. John then speaks of the
Judgment, referring essentially to the judgment of the wicked dead,
for the judgment of the righteous is past; they have already been

raised from the dead with bodies adapted to the glory they will inherit (see D&C 88:28–31). John stresses that *all* men, whether buried at sea or placed in the earth, will come forth from the dead to be judged according to their works. Jehovah declared anciently: "I the Lord search the heart, I try the reins, even to give every man according to his ways, and according to the fruit of his doings" (Jeremiah 17:10; see also Romans 2:6).

Salvation, or eternal life, comes to us as a gift—indeed, "the greatest of all the gifts of God" (D&C 6:13; 14:7). There is nothing any man or woman can do, no price they can pay, no bargain they can strike, that will purchase for them the highest of eternal rewards. It comes by the grace and goodness and merits and mercy of the Lord. It is, as Lehi explained to his son Jacob, free (2 Nephi 2:4; see also 2 Nephi 26:27). "Men and women unquestionably have impressive powers and can bring to pass great things," Elder Dallin H. Oaks has taught. "But after all our obedience and good works, we cannot be saved from death or the effects of our individual sins without the grace extended by the atonement of Jesus Christ. . . . In other words, salvation does not come simply by keeping the commandments. . . . Man cannot earn his own salvation."[7]

And yet, the kind and quality of life we will have hereafter—the glory we attain, the depth of happiness we enjoy, the kind of crown we wear—is a product of how we have lived, how we have manifested our faith through obedient discipleship (see James 2:19–20), how we have demonstrated our love and gratitude to God by keeping his commandments (see John 14:15). Those whose names are not found written in the Lamb's book of life, the book of the sealed and sanctified, suffer the second (and final spiritual) death.

9

A NEW HEAVEN AND
A NEW EARTH (21:1–22:5)

Revelation 21

Revelation 21 begins John's vision of the transfigured and renewed earth, even "a new heaven and a new earth" (v. 1). The
new earth is as it was in the beginning, for the land masses have
returned to their original places so that water no longer separates
islands and continents (see D&C 133:23–24). Next comes an exciting moment—the coming of the New Jerusalem, the holy city.
John beholds as it comes "down from God out of heaven, prepared
as a bride adorned for her husband" (v. 2). Zion from above (the
ancient city of Enoch) descends, while Zion from beneath (the
New Jerusalem on earth) is caught up unto God. The Lord said to
Enoch: "Then shalt thou and all thy city meet them there, and we
will receive them into our bosom, and they shall see us, and we will
fall upon their necks, and they shall fall upon our necks, and we
will kiss each other; and there shall be mine abode, and it shall be
Zion, which shall come forth out of all the creations which I have
made; and for the space of a thousand years the earth shall rest"
(Moses 7:63–64).

Revelation 21 is an excellent illustration of the fact that
each chapter does not necessarily follow the preceding one in
chronological order, so far as the future and the predicted events.
Notwithstanding, the Millennium is to be an unspeakably beautiful

day, for God will dwell with his people. There will be no tears, no sorrow, no pain, no death, for these things will have passed away (see vv. 3–4). It is a day when all the pure in heart will lift up their voices and sing together a *new song*:

> The Lord hath brought again Zion;
> The Lord hath redeemed his people, Israel,
> According to the election of grace,
> Which was brought to pass by the faith
> And covenant of their fathers.
> The Lord hath redeemed his people;
> And Satan is bound and time is no longer.
> The Lord hath gathered all things in one.
> The Lord hath brought down Zion from above.
> The Lord hath brought up Zion from beneath.
> The earth hath travailed and brought forth her strength;
> And truth is established in her bowels;
> And the heavens have smiled upon her;
> And she is clothed with the glory of her God;
> For he stands in the midst of his people.
> Glory, and honor, and power, and might,
> Be ascribed to our God; for he is full of mercy,
> Justice, grace and truth, and peace,
> Forever and ever, Amen. (D&C 84:99–102)

The Master Teacher speaks to John now, teaches by contrast, and explains that those who overcome the world will be given to drink the waters of life freely, will inherit all things (see also D&C 84:38), and will therefore become gods, meaning, the sons and daughters of God (see v. 7; D&C 76:58). But those who are faithless, unbelieving, liars, sorcerers, idolaters, whoremongers, and murderers—those who will inherit the telestial kingdom of glory (see v. 8; Revelation 22:15; D&C 76:103)—will suffer the torments of mental and spiritual anguish. "And they shall be servants of the Most High; but where God and Christ dwell they cannot come, worlds without end" (D&C 76:112).

One of the seven angels with vials of destruction (again, which of the seven we do not know) comes to John, carries him away in the Spirit to a high mountain, and shows him, in great detail, the city of New Jerusalem (see vv. 9–10). Revelation 21:11–27 and Revelation 22:1–5 tell of the appearance, dimensions, features, and glory of the city (much of the description is obviously symbolic):

1. The city is cubic in shape (see v. 16). "The city is thus more than square: it is a perfect cube. This shape is that of the Holy of Holies. It is the place where God dwells. There will be the added thought that God's people dwell there too in perfect fellowship with God. . . . Twelve thousand stadia is approximately 1,500 miles, the distance between London and Athens, between New York and Houston. . . . A city of this size is too large for the imagination to take in. John is certainly conveying the idea of splendour. And, more importantly, that of room for all."[1]

2. The streets are paved with "pure gold" and yet have the appearance of "transparent glass" (v. 21; see also D&C 130:9; 137:4). The gold symbolizes "the riches of eternity" (D&C 38:9; see also 6:7), while the transparent glass indicates that, as Habakkuk prophesied, "the earth shall be filled with the knowledge of the glory of the Lord, as the waters cover the sea" (Habakkuk 2:14; see also Isaiah 11:9).

3. There is no temple in the city, for the Father and the Son are the temple (see v. 22). We know from the prophetic word that temples of the Most High will continue to dot the earth and that during the Millennium the grand work of the redemption of souls will accelerate to a degree that we cannot now comprehend. To what extent temples will have a place and will continue to be

erected after the resurrection and glorification of the children of the Father is not known.

4. There is no need for the reflected luminaries such as the sun or the moon (see v. 23); the glory of God (the primary source of light) will light the New Jerusalem.

5. There is no night in the city and thus no reason to ever close the city gates (see v. 25). There is no ceiling on the number of saved beings, no upper limit on how many persons will be allowed to enter the holy city and be a part of the celestial community. Far more of our Heavenly Father's children will be saved than we suppose.

6. Those who inherit the city will be pure, and their names will be "written in the Lamb's book of life" (v. 27).

Revelation 22

7. A "pure river" gushing forth with the waters of life proceeds "out of the throne of God" (v. 1). How gloriously instructive is this blessed symbol! Jesus said, "He that believeth on me, as the scripture hath said, out of his belly shall flow rivers of living water" (John 7:38). And modern scripture says, "Unto him that keepeth my commandments I will give the mysteries of my kingdom, and the same shall be in him a well of living water, springing up unto everlasting life" (D&C 63:23).

8. In the middle of the street and on both sides of the river grows the tree of life, which produces "twelve manner of fruits" and yields fruit every month (v. 2). The "twelve manner of fruits" refers to "twelve crops in succession, not twelve kinds of fruit."[2] We remember that this fruit is "sweet above all that is sweet, and . . . white above all that is white, yea, and pure above all that is pure" (Alma 32:42).

The curse or restriction placed upon Adam and Eve (see Genesis 3:24) was that they were barred from partaking of the tree of life while yet in their sins. John sees the day when the curse of sin is gone and the restriction removed (see v. 3) so that all men and women have free access to "the love of God" (1 Nephi 11:22), the fruit that "is most precious and most desirable above all other fruits; yea, and it is the greatest of all the gifts of God" (1 Nephi 15:36).

9. Because Zion is "the pure in heart" (D&C 97:21), and because the pure in heart will see God (see Matthew 5:8), Zion consists of a society of people pure enough to enjoy the presence of God. God writes his name (see v. 4), or bestows godhood, on all such. See our discussion of the name of God on the forehead in Revelation 14.

10

EPILOGUE (22:6–21)

Overcome with awe as he considers the majesty, might, power, and glory of the Almighty, John falls down at the feet of the angel in a worshipful attitude. The angel quickly responds, "See thou do it not: for I am thy fellowservant, and of thy brethren the prophets, and of them which keep the sayings of this book: worship God" (vv. 8–9). John is then instructed not to seal the Revelation (see v. 10), for it is God's will that it be made known to those willing to ponder it prayerfully.

Then comes our Lord's testimony: "I Jesus have sent mine angel to testify unto you these things in the churches. I am the root and the offspring of David, and the bright and morning star" (v. 16; see also Matthew 22:42–45). Jesus is the root of David in that he is the Lord Jehovah, the God of Abraham, Isaac, and Jacob, the God who revealed himself to David. He is the offspring of David in the sense that when he came to earth as the Mortal Messiah—when he condescended to take a mortal tabernacle—he was born as a son of Mary, a descendant of Judah through David's kingly lineage. He is the bright and morning star in that he brings darkness to an end. After a long season of sorrow, he brings joy in the morning. "He is the light and the life of the world" (Mosiah 16:9; Alma 38:9; see also 3 Nephi 11:11).

A closing expression by John attests to the importance of the Apocalypse: "For I testify unto every man that heareth *the words of the prophecy of this book*, If any man shall add unto these things, God shall add unto him the plagues that are written in this book: and if any man shall take away from *the words of the book of this prophecy*, God shall take away his part out of the book of life, and out of the holy city, and from the things which are written in this book" (vv. 18–19; emphasis added). This clearly refers to someone tampering with the Apocalypse, the book of Revelation, just like the similar warning uttered by Moses against those who might add to or take away from his teachings in the fifth book of the Pentateuch (see Deuteronomy 4:2). God can and does choose to add to his divine word, and thanks be to him for it. He has given us the Holy Bible, and we rejoice in this sublime scriptural gem. But we dare not be arrogant or inappropriate in telling the Almighty what he can and cannot do by drawing a line in the sand and stating to our Father, "Thus far and no more." The words of Jesus Christ himself declare: "Wherefore murmur ye, because that ye shall receive more of my word? . . . Wherefore, because that ye have a Bible ye need not suppose that it contains all my words; neither need ye suppose that I have not caused more to be written" (2 Nephi 29:8, 10).

Jesus then certifies that he will "come quickly"—not necessarily soon but suddenly (see v. 20). Well might all who fear God—all who mourn over the sins of the world and who yearn to be a part of a world where honesty and integrity and modesty and decency and purity and holiness are the order of the day—join with John in a plea to the Son of Man, the King of Kings: "Even so, come, Lord Jesus" (v. 20).

Part Two
THE SECOND COMING
OF CHRIST

QUESTIONS AND ANSWERS

Because the signs of the times are such a central feature of John's revelation, it seems appropriate to devote a segment of this book to some of the most frequently asked questions about the Lord's second advent. We will lean heavily upon the Doctrine and Covenants for our scriptural support because it is a treasure house of doctrinal understanding.

What Is the Second Coming?

Jesus came to earth as a mortal being in the meridian of time. He taught the gospel, bestowed divine authority, organized the Church, and suffered and died as an infinite atoning sacrifice for the sins of the world. He stated that he would come again, would return not as the meek and lowly Nazarene but as the Lord of Sabaoth, the Lord of Hosts, the Lord of armies. His Second Coming is thus spoken of as his coming "in glory," meaning in his true identity as the God of all creation, the Redeemer and Judge. His Second Coming is described as both *great* and *dreadful*—great for those who have been true and faithful and who therefore look forward to his coming, and dreadful to those who have done despite to the spirit of grace and who therefore hope that he will never return. The Second Coming in glory is in fact "the end of the world," meaning the end of worldliness, "the destruction of the wicked" (Joseph Smith–Matthew 1:4, 31).[1] At his coming the wicked will be destroyed, the righteous quickened and caught up to meet him, and the earth transformed from a fallen telestial orb to a terrestrial, paradisiacal sphere. We will live and move about among new heavens and a new earth. The Second Coming will initiate the millennial reign.

Does Christ Himself Know When He Will Come?

This question comes up occasionally, perhaps because of what is stated in the Gospel of Mark: "Heaven and earth shall pass away: but my words shall not pass away. But of that day and that hour knoweth no man, no, not the angels which are in heaven, *neither the Son,* but the Father" (Mark 13:31–32; emphasis added). The phrase "neither the Son" is not found in Matthew or Luke. Christ knows all things; he possesses the "fulness of the glory" and power of the Father (see D&C 93:16–17). Surely he knows when he will return. It is worth noting that the Joseph Smith Translation of verse 32 (JST, Mark 13:47) omits the disputed phrase.

Will All Be Surprised and Caught Unaware?

The scriptures speak of the Master returning as "a thief in the night" (1 Thessalonians 5:2; 2 Peter 3:10). It is true that no mortal man has known, does now know, or will yet know the precise day of the Lord's second advent. That is true for prophets and apostles as well as the rank and file of society and the Church. The Lord did not reveal to Joseph Smith the precise day and time of his coming (see D&C 130:14–17). Elder M. Russell Ballard, speaking to students at Brigham Young University, said: "I am called as one of the Apostles to be a special witness of Christ in these exciting, trying times, and I do not know when He is going to come again. As far as I know, none of my brethren in the Quorum of the Twelve or even in the First Presidency knows. And I would humbly suggest that if we do not know, then *nobody* knows, no matter how compelling their arguments or how reasonable their calculations. . . .

"I believe that when the Lord says 'no one' knows, He really means that no one knows. We should be extremely wary of anyone who claims to be an exception to divine decree."[2]

On the other hand, the Saints are promised that if they are in tune with the Spirit, they can know the time and the season. The Apostle Paul chose the descriptive analogy of a pregnant woman about to deliver. She may not know the exact hour or day when the birth is to take place, but one thing she knows for sure: it will be soon. It *must* be soon! The impressions and feelings and signs within her body so testify. In that day, surely the Saints of the Most High, the members of the body of Christ, will be pleading for the Lord to deliver the travailing earth, to bring an end to corruption and degradation, to introduce an era of peace and righteousness. And those who give heed to the words of scripture, and especially to the living oracles, will stand as "the children of light, and the children of the day," those who "are not of the night, nor of darkness" (see 1 Thessalonians 5:2–5). In a modern revelation the Savior declared, "And again, verily I say unto you, the coming of the Lord draweth nigh, and *it overtaketh the world as a thief in the night*—therefore, gird up your loins, that you may be the children of light, and that day shall not overtake you as a thief" (D&C 106:4–5; emphasis added).

To certain brethren who would soon be called to the first Quorum of the Twelve Apostles in this dispensation, the Lord said,

"And unto you it shall be given to know the signs of the times, and the signs of the coming of the Son of Man" (D&C 68:11). As we move closer to the end of time, we would do well to live in such a manner that we can discern the signs of the times; we would be wise also to keep our eyes fixed and our ears riveted on those called to direct the destiny of the Church. The Prophet Joseph Smith pointed out that a particular man who claimed prophetic powers "has not seen the sign of the son of man as foretold by Jesus; neither has any man, nor will any man, till after the sun shall have been darkened and the moon bathed in blood, for the Lord hath not shown me any such sign, and, as the prophet saith, so it must be: *Surely the Lord God will do nothing, but he revealeth his secret unto his servants the prophets.*"[3]

Is It True That Not Everyone Will Know When the Savior Has Come?

Once in a while we hear something in the classes of the Church to the effect that not all people will know when the Lord returns. Let us be clear on this matter. There may be some wisdom in speaking of the second *comings* of the Lord Jesus Christ, three of which are preliminary appearances to select groups and one of which is to the whole world. The Lord will make a preliminary appearance to his temple in Independence, Jackson County, Missouri. This seems to be a private appearance to those holding the keys of power in the earthly kingdom. Elder Orson Pratt, in speaking of this appearance, said:

"All of them who are pure in heart will behold the face of the Lord and that too before he comes in his glory in the clouds of heaven, for he will suddenly come to his Temple, and he will purify the sons of Moses and of Aaron, until they shall be prepared to offer in that Temple an offering that shall be acceptable in the sight of the Lord. In doing this, he will purify not only the minds of the Priesthood in that Temple, but he will purify their bodies until they shall be quickened, renewed and strengthened, and they will be partially changed, not to immortality, but changed in part that they can be filled with the power of God, and they can stand in the presence of Jesus, and behold his face in the midst of that Temple."[4]

President Charles W. Penrose observed that the Saints "will come to the Temple prepared for him, and his faithful people will behold his face, hear his voice, and gaze upon his glory. From his own lips they will receive further instructions for the development and beautifying of Zion and for the extension and sure stability of his kingdom."[5]

The Lord will make an appearance at Adam-ondi-Ahman, "the place where Adam shall come to visit his people, or the Ancient of Days shall sit" (D&C 116:1). This grand council will be a large sacrament meeting, a time when the Son of Man will partake of the fruit of the vine once more with his earthly friends. And who will attend? The revelations specify Moroni, Elias, John the Baptist, Elijah, Abraham, Isaac, Jacob, Joseph, Adam, Peter, James, John, "and also," the Savior clarifies, "all those whom my Father hath given me out of the world" (D&C 27:5–14), multitudes of faithful Saints from the beginning of time to the end. This will be a private appearance in that it will be unknown to the world. It will be a leadership meeting, a time of accounting, an accounting for priesthood stewardships. The Prophet Joseph Smith explained that Adam, the Ancient of Days, "will call his children together and hold a council with them to prepare them for the coming of the Son of Man. He (Adam) is the father of the human family, and presides over the spirits of all men, and all that have had the keys must stand before him in this grand council. . . . The Son of Man stands before him, and there is given him [Christ] glory and dominion. Adam delivers up his stewardship to Christ, that which was delivered to him as holding the keys of the universe, but retains his standing as head of the human family."[6]

President Joseph Fielding Smith observed: "This gathering of the children of Adam, where the thousands, and the tens of thousands are assembled in the judgment, will be one of the greatest events this troubled earth has ever seen. At this conference, or council, all who have held keys of dispensations will render a report for their stewardship. . . . We do not know how long a time this gathering will be in session, or how many sessions may be held at this grand council. It is sufficient to know that it is a gathering of the Priesthood of God from the beginning of this earth down to the present, in which reports will be made and all who have been given dispensations (talents) will declare their keys and ministry and make report of their stewardship according to the parable [of the talents in Matthew 25]. Judgment will be rendered unto them[,] for this is a gathering of the righteous. . . . It is not to be the judgment of the wicked. . . . This will precede the great day of destruction of the wicked and will be the preparation for the Millennial Reign."[7]

Elder Bruce R. McConkie has likewise written: "Every prophet, apostle, president, bishop, elder, or church officer of whatever degree—all who have held keys shall stand before him who holds all of the keys. They will then be called upon to give an account of their stewardships and to report how and in what manner they have used their priesthood and their keys for the salvation of men within the sphere of their appointments. . . .

"There will be a great hierarchy of judges in that great day, of whom Adam, under Christ, will be the chief of all. Those judges will judge the righteous ones under their jurisdiction, but Christ himself, he alone, will judge the wicked."[8]

The Savior will appear to the Jews on the Mount of Olives. It will be at the time of the battle of Armageddon, when the Jews will find themselves with their backs against the wall. During this time, two prophets will stand before the wicked in the streets of Jerusalem and call the people to repentance. These men "are to be raised up to the Jewish nation in the last days, at the time of the restoration," and will "prophesy to the Jews after they are gathered and have built the city of Jerusalem in the land of their fathers" (D&C 77:15; see also Revelation 11:3–6). These prophets will be put to death by their enemies, their bodies will lie in the streets for three and a half days, and they will then be resurrected before the assembled multitude (see Revelation 11:7–12).

At about this time, the Savior will come to the rescue of his ancient covenant people: "Then shall the Lord go forth, and fight against those nations, as when he fought in the day of battle. And his feet shall stand in that day upon the mount of Olives, which is before Jerusalem on the east, and the mount of Olives shall cleave in the midst thereof toward the east and toward the west, and there shall be a very great valley; and half of the mountain shall remove toward the north, and half of it toward the south" (Zechariah 14:3–4).

Then will come to pass the conversion of a nation in a day, the acceptance of the Redeemer by the Jews. "And then shall the Jews look upon me and say: What are these wounds in thine hands and in thy feet? Then shall they know that I am the Lord; for I will say unto them: These wounds are the wounds with which I was wounded in the house of my friends. I am he who was lifted up. I am Jesus that was crucified. I am the Son of God. And then shall they weep because of their iniquities; then shall they lament because they persecuted their king" (D&C 45:51–53; see also Zechariah 12:10; 13:6).

Finally, and we would assume not far removed in time from his appearance on the Mount of Olives, is Christ's coming in glory. When he comes in glory, all will know. "Be not deceived," the

Master warned in a modern revelation, "but continue in steadfastness, looking forth for the heavens to be shaken, and the earth to tremble and to reel to and fro as a drunken man, and for the valleys to be exalted, and for the mountains to be made low, and for the rough places to become smooth" (D&C 49:23).

"Wherefore, prepare ye for the coming of the Bridegroom; go ye, go ye out to meet him. For behold, he shall stand upon the mount of Olivet, and upon the mighty ocean, even the great deep, and upon the islands of the sea, and upon the land of Zion. And he shall utter his voice out of Zion, and he shall speak from Jerusalem, and *his voice shall be heard among all people;* and it shall be a voice as the voice of many waters, and as the voice of a great thunder, which shall break down the mountains, and the valleys shall not be found" (D&C 133:19–22; emphasis added).

When the Lord Comes, Who Will Come with Him?

The righteous dead from ages past—those who qualify for the First Resurrection, specifically those who died true in the faith since the time the First Resurrection was initiated in the meridian of time—will come with the Savior when he returns in glory. The Prophet Joseph corrected a passage in Paul's first epistle to the Thessalonians as follows:

"I would not have you to be ignorant, brethren, concerning them which are asleep, that ye sorrow not, even as others which have no hope. For if we believe that Jesus died and rose again, even so them also which sleep in Jesus will God bring with him. For this we say unto you by the word of the Lord, that they who are alive at the coming of the Lord, shall not prevent [precede] them who remain unto the coming of the Lord, who are asleep. For the Lord himself shall descend from heaven with a shout, with the voice of the archangel, and with the trump of God: and the dead in Christ shall rise first: Then they who are alive, shall be caught up together into the clouds with them who remain, to meet the Lord in the air; and so shall we be ever with the Lord" (JST, 1 Thessalonians 4:13–17).

What Happens to Those Living on Earth When He Comes?

Those who are of at least a terrestrial level of righteousness will continue to live as mortals after the Lord returns. The Saints will live to "the age of man" (D&C 63:50)—in the words of Isaiah, the age of one hundred (Isaiah 65:20)—and will then pass through death and be changed instantly from mortality to resurrected immortality. "Yea, and blessed are the dead that die in the Lord, . . . when the Lord shall come, and old things shall pass away, and all things become new, they shall rise from the dead and shall not die after, and shall receive an inheritance before the Lord, in the holy city. And he that liveth when the Lord shall come, and hath kept the faith, blessed is he; nevertheless, it is appointed to him to die at the age of man. Wherefore, children shall grow up until they become old"—meaning no longer will little ones die before the time of accountability; "old men shall die; but they shall not sleep in the dust, but they shall be changed in the twinkling of an eye" (D&C 63:49–51; see also Isaiah 65:20).

President Joseph Fielding Smith pointed out that "the inhabitants of the earth will be and have a sort of translation. They will be transferred to a condition of the terrestrial order, and so they will have power over disease and they will have power to live until they get a certain age and then they will die."[9]

Is the Burning Spoken of in Scripture Literal?

Malachi prophesied that "the day cometh, that shall burn as an oven; and all the proud, yea, and all that do wickedly, shall be stubble: and the day that cometh shall burn them up, saith the Lord of hosts, that it shall leave them neither root nor branch" (Malachi 4:1; see also 2 Nephi 26:4; D&C 133:64). In 1823 Moroni quoted this passage differently to the seventeen-year-old Joseph Smith: "And all the proud, yea, and all that do wickedly shall burn as stubble; for *they that come* shall burn them, saith the Lord of Hosts" (Joseph Smith–History 1:37; emphasis added).

In the Doctrine and Covenants the Lord declares, "For the hour is nigh and the day soon at hand when the earth is ripe; and all the proud and they that do wickedly shall be as stubble; and *I will burn them up*, saith the Lord of Hosts, that wickedness shall not be upon the earth" (D&C 29:9; emphasis added), "For after today cometh the burning," a day wherein "all the proud and they that do wickedly shall be as stubble; and *I will burn them up*, for I am the Lord of Hosts; and I will not spare any that remain in Babylon" (D&C 64:24; emphasis added).

The Second Coming of Christ in glory is a day in which "every corruptible thing, both of man, or of the beasts of the field, or of the fowls of the heavens, or of the fish of the sea, that dwells upon all the face of the earth, shall be consumed; and also that of element shall melt with fervent heat; and all things shall become new, that my knowledge and glory may dwell upon all the earth" (D&C 101:24–25; see also 133:41; 2 Peter 3:10).

President Joseph Fielding Smith wrote: "Somebody said, 'Brother Smith, do you mean to say that it is going to be literal fire?' I said, 'Oh, no, it will not be literal fire any more than it was literal water that covered the earth in the flood.'"[10]

Why Will the Savior Appear in Red Apparel?

Red is symbolic of victory—victory over the devil, death, hell, and endless torment—and symbolic of "being placed beyond the power of all [one's] enemies."[11] Christ's red apparel will also symbolize both aspects of his ministry to fallen humanity—his mercy and his justice. Because he has trodden the winepress alone, "even the wine-press of the fierceness of the wrath of Almighty God" (D&C 76:107; 88:106), he has descended below all things and mercifully taken upon him our stains, our blood, and our sins (see 2 Nephi 9:44; Jacob 1:19; 2:2; Alma 5:22). In addition, he comes in "dyed garments" (D&C 133:46) as the God of justice, even he who has trampled the wicked beneath his feet.

"And the Lord shall be red in his apparel, and his garments like him that treadeth in the wine-vat. And so great shall be the glory of his presence that the sun shall hide his face in shame, and the moon shall withhold its light, and the stars shall be hurled from their places. And his voice shall be heard: I have trodden the winepress alone, and have brought judgment upon all people; and none were with me; and I have trampled them in my fury, and I did tread upon them in mine anger, and their blood have I sprinkled upon my garments, and stained all my raiment; for this was the day of vengeance which was in my heart" (D&C 133:48–51).

When Does the Millennium Begin? Why Will It Begin?

The Second Coming in glory of Jesus Christ ushers in the Millennium. The Millennium does not begin when Christ comes to his temple in Missouri, when he appears at Adam-ondi-Ahman, or when he stands on the Mount of Olives in Jerusalem. The

Millennium will not come because men and women on earth have become noble and good or because Christian charity will have spread across the globe and goodwill is the order of the day. The Millennium will not come because technological advances and medical miracles will have extended human life or because peace treaties among warring nations will have soothed injured feelings and eased political tensions for a time. The Millennium will be brought in by power, by the power of him who is King of Kings and Lord of Lords. Satan will be bound by power, and the glory of the Millennium will be maintained by the righteousness of those who are permitted to live on earth (see 1 Nephi 22:15, 26).

What Are the Times of the Gentiles, the Fulness of the Gentiles?

In the meridian of time, by command of the Savior, the gospel of Jesus Christ was delivered first to the Jews and later to the Gentiles. In our day the gospel was delivered first to Joseph Smith and the Latter-day Saints, those of us who are "identified with the Gentiles" (D&C 109:60), those who are Israelite by descent (D&C 52:2; 86:8–10) and Gentile by culture. The gospel is given to us, and we bear the responsibility to take the message of the Restoration to the descendants of Lehi and to the Jews (see 1 Nephi 22:7–11). We therefore live in "the times of the Gentiles."

"And when the times of the Gentiles is come in, a light shall break forth among them that sit in darkness, and it shall be the fulness of my gospel" (D&C 45:28). It is a time, in the words of Elder Marion G. Romney, in which "in this last dispensation, the gospel is to be preached primarily to the non-Jewish people of the earth."[12]

In a future day, a time when the Gentiles—presumably those outside the Church as well as some from within the fold—sin against the fulness of the gospel and reject its supernal blessings, the Lord will take away these privileges from the Gentile nations and once again make them available primarily to his ancient covenant people (see 3 Nephi 16:10–11). This will be known as "the fulness of the times of the Gentiles" or simply "the fulness of the Gentiles" (3 Nephi 16:4; Romans 11:25). The people of earth will no longer receive the light of gospel fulness and will "turn their hearts from [the Lord] because of the precepts of men. And in that generation shall the times of the Gentiles be fulfilled" (D&C 45:29–30). In the purest sense, this will not take place until Jesus sets his foot upon Olivet and the Jews acknowledge their long-awaited Messiah. Thus the fulness of the Gentiles is millennial.[13]

What Are We to Expect Regarding the Return of the Ten Tribes?

As we all know, there have been numerous legends, traditions, vague reminiscences, and myriad folktales that deal with the location and eventual return of the lost ten tribes, those from the northern part of Israel who were taken captive by the Assyrians in 721 B.C. The Book of Mormon teaches that the ten tribes are scattered among the nations, lost as much to their identity as to their whereabouts (see 1 Nephi 22:3–4). Thus it seems that the restoration, or gathering, of the ten tribes consists in scattered Israel—descendants of Jacob from such tribes as Reuben, Gad, Asher, Naphtali, Zebulun, and, of course, Joseph—coming "to the knowledge of their Redeemer," accepting Christ's gospel (see 1 Nephi 15:14), coming into "the true church and fold of God" (2 Nephi 9:2), congregating with the faithful, and receiving the ordinances of the house of the Lord.[14] That is to say, the ten tribes will be gathered as all others are gathered—through conversion.

The risen Lord explained to the Nephites that after his Second Coming, once he has begun to dwell on earth with his faithful, "then shall the work of the Father"—the work of the gathering of Israel—"commence at that day, even when this gospel shall be preached among the remnant of this people. Verily I say unto you, at that day shall the work of the Father commence among all the dispersed of my people, yea, even the tribes which have been lost, which the Father hath led away out of Jerusalem" (see 3 Nephi 21:25–26). It will *commence* in the sense that it will be of such magnitude as to cause earlier efforts at gathering to pale into insignificance.

The return of the ten tribes is spoken of in modern revelation in majestic symbolism: "And the Lord, even the Savior, shall stand in the midst of his people, and shall reign over all flesh" (D&C 133:25). Further, those who are descendants of the northern tribes will respond to the gospel message, come under the direction of those prophets or priesthood leaders in their midst, traverse that highway we know as the "way of holiness" (Isaiah 35:8), and eventually participate in temple ordinances that prepare them to be kings and queens, priests and priestesses unto God; they will "fall down and be crowned with glory, even in Zion, by the hands of the servants of the Lord, even the children of Ephraim," those who are entrusted with the keys of salvation (D&C 133:26–32).[15]

In addition to that portion of the record of the ten tribes in our possession that we know as the Doctrine and Covenants—the record of God's dealings with modern Ephraim—we thrill in the assurance that other sacred volumes chronicling our Redeemer's ministry to the lost tribes will come forth during the Millennium (2 Nephi 29:13).

Must Every Person Living on Earth Hear the Gospel before the Lord Can Come?

In November 1831 the early elders of the Church were authorized to preach the gospel: "Go ye into all the world, preach the gospel to every creature, acting in the authority which I have given you, baptizing in the name of the Father, and of the Son, and of the Holy Ghost" (D&C 68:8). "For, verily, the sound must go forth from this place into all the world, and unto the uttermost parts of the earth—the gospel must be preached unto every creature, with signs following them that believe" (D&C 58:64). It is true that every person must have the opportunity to hear the gospel, either here or hereafter. Eventually "the truth of God will go forth boldly, nobly, and independent, till it has penetrated every continent, visited every clime, swept every country, and sounded in every ear, till the purposes of God shall be accomplished, and the Great Jehovah shall say the work is done."[16]

Not all people, however, will have that privilege as mortals, and not all will have that privilege before the Second Coming. Jesus spoke to the Twelve about the last days as follows: "And again, this Gospel of the Kingdom shall be preached in all the world, for a witness unto all nations, and then shall the end come, or the destruction of the wicked" (Joseph Smith–Matthew 1:31). As we have seen, the great day of gathering—the day when millions upon millions will come into the true fold of God—is millennial. But there is more. Elder McConkie explained that before Jesus can return in glory, two things must take place:

"The first . . . is that the restored gospel is to be preached in every nation and among every people and to those speaking every tongue. Now there is one immediate reaction to this: Can't we go on the radio and preach the gospel to . . . [the] nations of the earth? We certainly can, but that would have very little bearing on the real meaning of the revelation that says we must preach it to every nation, kindred, and people. The reason is the second thing that must occur before the second coming: The revelations expressly, specifically, and pointedly say that when the Lord comes the second time to usher in the millennial era, he is going to find, in every nation, kindred, and tongue, and among every people, those who are kings and queens, who will live and reign a thousand years on earth. (Revelation 5:9–10)

"That is a significant statement that puts in perspective the preaching of the gospel to the world. Yes, we can go on the radio; we can proclaim the gospel to all nations by television or other modern invention. And to the extent that we do it, so be it, it's all to the good. But that's not what is involved. What is involved is that the elders of Israel, holding the priesthood, in person have to tread the soil, eat in the homes of the people, figuratively put their arms around the honest in heart, feed them the gospel, and baptize them and confer the Holy Ghost upon them. Then these people have to progress and advance, and grow in the things of the Spirit, until they can go to the house of the Lord, until they can enter a temple of God and receive the blessings of the priesthood, out of which come the rewards of being kings and priests.

"The way we become kings and priests is through the ordinances of the house of the Lord. It is through celestial marriage; it is through the guarantees of eternal life and eternal increase that are reserved for the Saints in the temples. The promise is that when the Lord comes he is going to find in every nation and kindred, among every people speaking every tongue, those who will, at that hour of his coming, have already become kings and priests. . . . All this is to precede the second coming of the Son of Man."[17]

Who Are the False Christs and False Prophets?

We must keep our eyes fixed on those charged with the direction of the Church—the prophets, seers, and revelators of our day. What they stress in their instruction to us should be what we stress. Those who come before the Saints claiming some special insight, gift, training, or commission to elucidate detail concerning the signs of the times beyond that which the Brethren have set forth are suspect, are running before their leaders. Teachings from such people are not to be trusted or received. Truly, "it shall not be given to any one to go forth to preach my gospel, or to build up my church, except he be ordained by some one who has authority, and it is known to the church that he has authority and has been regularly ordained by the heads of the church" (D&C 42:11).

With the exception of those few deluded persons who claim to be Jesus, when we speak of false Christs, we speak not so much of individuals as of false spirits, false doctrines, and false systems of salvation. Latter-day Saints who "stick with the Brethren"[18] and who study and teach from the conference reports, the official pronouncements and proclamations, and the monthly First Presidency messages in the *Ensign* are they who treasure up the word of the Lord and will not be deceived or led astray at the last day (see Joseph Smith–Matthew 1:37). Elder Boyd K. Packer declared: "There are some among us now who have *not* been regularly ordained by the heads of the Church and who tell of impending political and economic chaos, the end of the world. . . .

"Those deceivers say that the Brethren do not know what is going on in the world or that the Brethren approve of their teaching but do not wish to speak of it over the pulpit. Neither is true. The Brethren, by virtue of traveling constantly everywhere on earth, certainly know what is going on, and by virtue of prophetic insight are able to read the signs of the times."[19]

What Are the Best Sources for Understanding the Events Incident to the Savior's Coming?

At the October 1972 general conference of the Church, President Harold B. Lee warned Latter-day Saints about what he called "loose writings," presumably from within and outside the Church in regard to the signs of the times. "Are you . . . aware of the fact," President Lee inquired, "that we need no such publications to be forewarned, if we were only conversant with what the scriptures have already spoken to us in plainness?" He then provided what he termed "the sure word of prophecy on which [we] should rely for [our] guide instead of these strange sources." He instructed the Saints to read the Joseph Smith Translation of Matthew 24 (what we have in the Pearl of Great Price as Joseph Smith–Matthew) and sections 38, 45, 101, and 133 of the Doctrine and Covenants.[20] It is interesting that President Lee cited primarily the revelations of the Restoration.

Even given the divine direction of living oracles and the words of sacred scripture brought forth in this final age, we really cannot plot or calculate the signs of the times or lay out a precise scheme of events. As one Apostle pointed out, "It is not possible for us . . . to specify the exact chronology of all the events that shall attend the Second Coming. Nearly all of the prophetic word relative to our Lord's return links various events together without reference to the order of their occurrence. Indeed, the same scriptural language is often used to describe similar events that will take place at different times."[21]

Conclusion

We could go on and on, but these feeble efforts at providing answers point us to the glorious reality that modern revelation represents, in the language of Elder Parley P. Pratt, "the dawning of a brighter day."[22] Instructing the early elders of the Church, the Lord said, "Wherefore, be of good cheer, and do not fear, for I the Lord am with you, and will stand by you; and ye shall bear record of me, even Jesus Christ, that I am the Son of the living God, that I was, that I am, and that I am to come" (D&C 68:6). Answer after divine answer concerning such matters as the divine sonship of Christ, his infinite and eternal atoning sacrifice, the principles of his eternal gospel—these things are made known with great power and persuasion. In addition, the revelations testify that:

- Jesus will come again to reign among the Saints and to "come down in judgment upon Idumea, or the world" (see D&C 1:36).

- He will gather his faithful as a mother hen and enable them to "partake of the waters of life" (see D&C 10:65–66; 29:2; 33:6).

- Satan and the works of Babylon will be destroyed (see D&C 1:16; 19:3; 35:11).

- This dispensation of the gospel represents his last pruning of the vineyard (see D&C 24:19; 33:2–3; 39:17; 43:28).

- The elect in the last days will hear his voice; they will not be asleep because they will be purified (see D&C 35:20–21).

- We will have no laws but his laws when he comes; he will be our ruler (see D&C 38:22; 41:4; 58:22).

- From the Lord's perspective, according to his reckoning, his coming is nigh (see D&C 63:53); he comes tomorrow (see D&C 64:24); he comes quickly, suddenly (see D&C 33:18; 35:27; 36:8; 39:24; 41:4; 68:35).

That we will follow the Brethren, search the scriptures, pray mightily for discernment and awareness and understanding of the signs of the times is my hope. That we will be wise, receive the truth, take the Holy Spirit for our guide, and thereby have our lamps filled (see D&C 45:57) is my prayer. "Wherefore, be faithful, praying always, having your lamps trimmed and burning, and oil with you, that you may be ready at the coming of the Bridegroom— for behold, verily, verily, I say unto you, that I come quickly" (D&C 33:17–18).

Part Three
THE MILLENNIUM

THE MILLENNIUM

It is easy in our busy and complex world to become ensnared by programs, points of view, and ways of life that have no lasting value, no everlasting import. We are eternal beings involved in a mortal experience, and one of the tasks of this estate is to see to it that we do not become preoccupied with the ephemeral, that which is wholly temporal, that which will eventually pass away. We live in a day of wickedness and vengeance, an era in this world's temporal continuance when Satan, the god of the worldly, rages in the hearts of men and women. But we look upon the present distress with an eye of faith, with an eye to the future, with the certain assurance that one day soon the God of all will bring an abrupt end to unholiness and inaugurate an age of peace and happiness. In a not-too-distant day, the light of the great Millennium will dawn, and things will be very different on this earth.

The First Resurrection Resumes

On the day "the face of the Lord shall be unveiled," then "the saints that are upon the earth, who are alive, shall be quickened and be caught up to meet him" (D&C 88:95–96). That quickening would seem to entail the accentuation of man's spiritual nature and the subduing of his fallen nature. Elder Orson Pratt explained that "all the inhabitants who are spared from this fire—those who are not proud, and who do not do wickedly—will be cleansed more fully and filled with the glory of God. A partial change will be wrought upon them"—a type of translation—"not a change to immortality, like that which all the Saints will undergo when they are changed in the twinkling of an eye, from mortality to immortality; but so great will be the change then wrought that the children who are born into the world will grow up without sin unto salvation [see D&C 45:58]. Why will this be so? Because *that fallen nature, introduced by the fall, and transferred from parents to children, from generation to generation, will be, in a measure, eradicated by this change.*"[1]

The First Resurrection began with the resurrection of Christ in the meridian of time. All of the prophets and those who gave heed to the words of the prophets, from the days of Adam to Christ—and, we would presume, all those who never had an opportunity to hear the gospel but would have received it had they been given the privilege (see D&C 137:7–9)—came forth from the grave some time after the Savior's rise to immortal glory (Mosiah 15:21–25; Alma 40:20). We have no indication that there has been a wholesale resurrection of Saints since the resurrection of the Savior.

"There are some who feel," President Ezra Taft Benson pointed out, "that the resurrection is going on continually and has been since that time. That is not scripturally true, but we do know that it is possible for our Father to call from the graves those whom He needs to perform special missions and special service. For example, we know of at least three [Peter, James, and Moroni] who have been called up since the resurrection of the Master and since that first mass resurrection when the graves were opened and many of the Saints arose."[2]

When the Master returns in glory to take charge of affairs on this earth, with him will come a host of the righteous dead. The

First Resurrection will thereby resume. Those who have died true to the faith, who were valiant in the testimony of Jesus, and who kept the celestial law will return to earth with resurrected, immortal bodies.

"They who have slept in their graves shall come forth, for their graves shall be opened; and they also shall be caught up to meet him in the midst of the pillar of heaven—They are Christ's, the first fruits, they who shall descend with him first, and they who are on the earth and in their graves, who are first caught up to meet him" (D&C 88:97–98). Or, according to the testimony of the Apostle Paul, "they who are alive"—meaning, presumably, physically alive when the Lord comes—"shall be caught up together into the clouds with them who remain, to meet the Lord in the air; and so shall we be ever with the Lord" (JST, 1 Thessalonians 4:17).

The Lord of the living and the dead "will come with ten thousands of his saints, all of them resurrected persons from ages past. He will call forth from their graves and from the watery deep ten thousands of his other saints, all of them righteous persons who have lived since his mortal ministry. Those among his saints on earth who are faithful will be caught up to meet him in the clouds of glory, and they will then return to earth with him to live out their appointed days on the new earth with its new heavens."[3] This is the First Resurrection, or, as we have come to call it, the morning of the First Resurrection, the resurrection of the celestial.

With Christ will come the hosts of persons who were translated before the resurrection of Christ, those who were taken into terrestrial glory without tasting death. Enoch and Melchizedek with their cities, Elijah and Moses and Alma and Nephi, and, surely, congregations and communities of the pure in heart of which we have no knowledge will return as resurrected personages. These were with Christ in his resurrection (see D&C 133:54–55).[4] Those who have been translated since the resurrection of Christ—John the Beloved, the three Nephites, and other holy men or women we "know not of" (D&C 49:8)—will undergo the "change equivalent to death" and be transformed instantaneously from their translated mortal state to resurrected immortality at the time of our Savior's return in glory (see 3 Nephi 28:8).[5]

Although men and women who are alive at the time of Christ's Second Coming will be changed and quickened, they will yet continue to live as mortals. For them, death and immortality lie ahead. The mortal Saints will live to "the age of man" (D&C 63:50) during the Millennium, what Isaiah explained to be one hundred years (see Isaiah 65:20). At that point they will pass instantly from mortality through death into resurrected immortality "in the twinkling of an eye" (1 Corinthians 15:52; 3 Nephi 28:8). For these there will be no time for the body in the grave and no sojourn in the postmortal world of spirits, for they will be received into glory immediately after their death: "Wherefore, children shall grow up until they become old; old men shall die; but they shall not sleep in the dust, but they shall be changed in the twinkling of an eye" (D&C 63:51).

"During the Millennium," Elder Bruce R. McConkie wrote, "there will, of course, be two kinds of people on earth. There will be those who are mortal, and those who are immortal. There will be those who have been changed or quickened or transfigured or translated (words fail us to describe their state), and those who have gone through a second change, in the twinkling of an eye, so as to become eternal in nature. There will be those who are on probation, for whom earth life is a probationary estate, and who [as mortals] are thus working out their own salvation, and those who have already overcome the world and have entered into a fulness of eternal joy. There will be those who will yet die in the sense of being changed from their quickened state to a state of immortality, and those who, having previously died, are then living in a resurrected state. There will be those who are subject to the kings and priests who rule forever in the house of Israel, and those who, as kings and priests, exercise power and dominion in the everlasting kingdom of Him whose we are. There will be those who, as mortals, provide bodies for the spirit children of the Father, for the spirits whose right it is to come to earth and gain houses for their eternal spirits, and those who, as immortals (Abraham is one), are already begetting spirit children of their own. There will be those for whom the fulness of eternal glory is ahead, and those who, again like Abraham, have already entered into their exaltation and sit upon their thrones and are not angels but are gods forever and ever."[6]

Why it is that certain persons, surely billions of our brothers and sisters, will be sent to earth to gain their mortal and then immortal bodies during this glorious era—an era during which they will not be tested, at least in the same ways we are now—is not known. This we do know: our God is perfectly just, he is perfectly merciful, and he is impartial. He is no respecter of persons and delights in the development and ultimate salvation of all his sons and daughters. He is all-wise and all-knowing, and thus we would assume that he would arrange and orchestrate the times and seasons and events of our lives in such a way as to maximize our growth and further our spirituality. The Saints of the Most High ought to glory in the knowledge that so many could come to the earth and be born, be nurtured in an Edenic atmosphere, and grow up without sin unto salvation.

The Growing Glory of the Millennium

When the telestial elements are stripped away from this orb, when sin and iniquity are burned away by the brightness of the coming of the King of Zion, the wickedness that befouls the planet will be no more and earth will rest. No longer will mother earth cry out in painful weariness because of the pollutions upon her surface (see Moses 7:48; see also Romans 8:22), for the stains of willful sin will have been purged out, and the glory of heaven will be felt by every person. The Savior will be in our midst (see 3 Nephi 20:22; 21:25). He will reign over Zion and minister among his chosen people in both the Old Jerusalem and the New Jerusalem. He will dwell among his Saints, teach them in their congregations, and see to it that his doctrine is declared from one end of the earth to the other.

Not all who inhabit the earth during the beginning of the Millennium, however, will be of one faith and one baptism. In that early hour of millennial splendor, not all will be converted to The Church of Jesus Christ of Latter-day Saints. Inasmuch as the terrestrial of the earth, those who are honorable and good, who are kindly and well-disposed, will be spared the burning, they will live and move and have their being on the same earth as the members of the household of faith. Seeing is often not believing. Just as men and women are actuated and driven in this life by their faith and quest for the fulness of truth, so also will men and women of a millennial kind be likewise driven and motivated. And just as noble and upright souls in all nations and climes hesitate in our day to partake of the glories of the new and everlasting covenant, so also will many refuse the fulness of gospel light in that day when the Mediator of the new covenant presides among his Saints.

President Brigham Young stated: "If the Latter-day Saints think, when the kingdom of God is established on the earth, that all the inhabitants of the earth will join the church called Latter-day Saints, they are egregiously mistaken. I presume there will be as many sects and parties then as now."[7] On another occasion President Young said: "When Jesus comes to rule and reign King of Nations as he now does King of Saints, the veil of the covering will be taken from all nations, that *all flesh may see his glory together, but that will not make them all Saints.* Seeing the Lord does not make a man a Saint, seeing an Angel does not make a man a Saint by any means."

President Young then added that in that day "kings and potentates of the nations will come up to Zion to inquire after the ways of the Lord, and to seek out the great knowledge, wisdom, and understanding manifested through the Saints of the Most High. They will inform the people of God that they belong to such and such a Church, and do not wish to change their religion."[8] In short, "In the millennium men will have the privilege of being Presbyterians, Methodists or Infidels, but they will not have the privilege of treating the name and character of Deity as they have done heretofore. No, but every knee shall bow and every tongue confess to the glory of God the Father that Jesus is the Christ."[9]

And yet the testimony of the scriptures and the prophets is consistent that as the power of God's Spirit continues to spread, eventually "the earth shall be full of the knowledge of the Lord, as the waters cover the sea" (Isaiah 11:9; see also Habakkuk 2:14). Truly "in that day when the Lord shall come, he shall reveal all things—things which have passed, and hidden things which no man knew, things of the earth, by which it was made, and the purpose and the end thereof—things most precious, things that are above, and things that are beneath, things that are in the earth, and upon the earth, and in heaven" (D&C 101:32–34).

"The gospel will be taught," President Joseph Fielding Smith observed, "far more intensely and with greater power during the millennium, *until all the inhabitants of the earth shall embrace it.* . . . Through the revelations given to the prophets, we learn that during the reign of Jesus Christ for a thousand years *eventually all people will embrace the truth.*"[10]

The Prophet Joseph Smith, drawing upon the prophecies in Zechariah, said, "There will be wicked men on the earth during the thousand years." By *wicked* he presumably meant those of a terrestrial order, those who will refuse to come unto the Father through receiving the fulness of his gospel (see Zechariah 14:16–18; see also D&C 84:49–53; 35:12).[11] The Prophet's statement continues: "The heathen nations who will not come up to worship will be visited with the judgments of God, and must eventually be destroyed from the earth."[12]

Isaiah testified, "In those days there shall be no more thence an infant of days, nor an old man that hath not filled his days; for the child shall not die, but shall live to be an hundred years old; but *the sinner, living to be an hundred years old, shall be accursed*" (JST, Isaiah 65:20; emphasis added). Elder McConkie similarly explained that "there will be many churches on earth when the Millennium begins. False worship will continue among those whose desires are good, 'who are honorable men of the earth,' but who have been 'blinded by the craftiness of men.' (D&C 76:75.) Plagues will rest upon them until they repent and believe the gospel or are destroyed, as the Prophet said. It follows that missionary work will continue into the Millennium until all who remain are converted. . . . Then every living soul on earth will belong to The Church of Jesus Christ of Latter-day Saints."[13]

Daily Life

We can only imagine such an existence—a life without physical pain and premature death, an existence without the sorrow that accompanies sin and waywardness, a time without the disappointment associated with dishonesty and greed. Isaiah proclaimed that in that day "the wolf also shall dwell with the lamb, and the leopard shall lie down with the kid; and the calf and the young lion and the fatling together; and a little child shall lead them. And the cow and the bear shall feed; their young ones shall lie down together: and the lion shall eat straw like the ox. And the sucking child shall play on the hole of the asp, and the weaned child shall put his hand on the cockatrice' den. They shall not hurt nor destroy in all my holy mountain" (Isaiah 11:6–9; see also 65:25). "In that day the enmity of man, and the enmity of beasts, yea, the enmity of all flesh"—an animosity, a natural tension and unrest that resulted from the Fall—"shall cease from before my face" (D&C 101:26). And so it is that "violence shall no more be heard in thy land, wasting nor destruction within thy borders; but thou shalt call thy walls Salvation, and thy gates Praise" (Isaiah 60:18).

Mortals will inhabit the earth alongside immortals during the entirety of the thousand years. Men and women who abide the day of the Lord's coming in glory will continue to live on this earth in an Edenic state. They will labor and study and grow and interact and love and socialize as before, but such things will be undertaken in a totally moral environment.

"When the Savior shall appear," the Prophet Joseph Smith taught, "we shall see him as he is. We shall see that he is a man like ourselves. And *that same sociality which exists among us here will exist among us there, only it will be coupled with eternal glory, which glory we do not now enjoy*" (D&C 130:1–2; emphasis added). "And they shall build houses, and inhabit them; and they shall plant vineyards, and eat the fruit of them. They shall not build, and another inhabit; they shall not plant, and another eat" (Isaiah 65:21–22). In other words, in the Millennium men and women will enjoy the fruits of their labors. In a world where there is no extortion, no bribery, no organized crime, where there are no unjust laws, no class distinctions of men and women according to income or chances for learning, people will no longer be preyed upon by the perverse or the malicious or forced to relocate because of financial demands or pressures. Our longings for stability, for longevity, and for permanence will be largely satisfied, for the father of lies and those who have spread his influence will have no place on the earth during the thousand years.

"Now, how will it be on this earth when Christ reigns?" President George Q. Cannon inquired. "When the Millennium dawns, Satan bound and the elements of the earth at our disposal and under our control, there will be no hunger, no thirst, no nakedness, no vagrants, no houseless people; *all will have that which is necessary to supply their physical wants. But there will be no waste.* One man will not be allowed to lord it over another and take possession of more than he needs; but *all will have a fulness,* Satan will be bound. He will not have power to inflict the misery he has done and is doing."[14]

The Great Day of Temple Work

The work of gathering people into the fold is not complete when they are baptized and confirmed members of The Church of Jesus Christ of Latter-day Saints. The final phase of this divine process consists of gathering to holy temples to be endowed with power from on high and receiving therein the ordinances of exaltation.[15] It follows that because millions upon millions of souls will join themselves to the Saints in the Millennium, temple work will be among the most significant labor performed.

President Wilford Woodruff taught that "this work of administering the ordinances of the house of God to the dead . . . will require the whole of the Millennium, with Jesus at the head of the resurrected dead to attend to it."[16] President Joseph F. Smith likewise observed that "the great work of the Millennium shall be the work in the temples for the redemption of the dead; and then, we hope to enjoy the benefits of revelation through the Urim and Thummim, or by such means as the Lord may reveal concerning those for whom the work shall be done."[17]

The scriptures attest that there will be kings and priests in every land and among every kindred, tongue, and people before the Lord Jesus comes in glory (see Revelation 5:9–10). That implies that temples will dot the earth, that the fulness of priesthood blessings will be available to men and women everywhere, even before the ushering in of the Millennium. Such sacred labor will be intensified during the thousand-year era of peace and righteousness, for *"to accomplish this work there will have to be not only one temple but thousands of them,* and thousands and tens of thousands of men and women will go into those temples and officiate for people who have lived as far back as the Lord shall reveal."[18]

We suppose that the work of the Church and kingdom of God—the establishment of men, women, and children in eternal family units through the powers of the holy priesthood—will come to complete fruition by the end of the Millennium. When, by the end of the thousand years, people of the Church will have achieved a "unity of the faith," the Church of Jesus Christ, as we know it now, will have served its function (Ephesians 4:11–15). What church or ecclesiastical system of organization will exist in eternity, beyond the patriarchal order (see Moses 6:7), has not been made known. As to the ordinances and work of the Church during the thousand years, Elder McConkie has suggested:

"During the Millennium children will be named and blessed by the elders of the kingdom. When those of the rising generation arrive at the years of accountability, they will be baptized in water and of the Spirit by legal administrators appointed so to act. Priesthood will be conferred upon young and old, and they will be ordained to offices therein as the needs of the ministry and their own salvation require. At the appropriate time each person will receive his patriarchal blessing, we suppose from the natural patriarch who presides in his family, as it was in Adamic days and as it was when Jacob blessed his sons. The saints will receive their endowments in the temples of the Lord, and they will receive the blessings of celestial marriage at their holy altars. And all of the faithful will have their callings and elections made sure and will be sealed up unto that eternal life which will come to them when they reach the age of a tree. We see no reasons why the ordinances of administering to the sick or the dedication of graves should continue, for disease and death shall be no more."[19]

We sing an anthem of praise and anticipation, a hymn that points our minds toward the glorious days ahead:

> The day dawn is breaking, the world is awaking,
> The clouds of night's darkness are fleeing away.
> The worldwide commotion, from ocean to ocean,
> Now heralds the time of the beautiful day.
>
> In many a temple the Saints will assemble
> And labor as saviors of dear ones away.
> Then happy reunion and sweetest communion
> We'll have with our friends in the beautiful day.
>
> Still let us be doing, our lessons reviewing,
> Which God has revealed for our walk in his way;
> And then, wondrous story, the Lord in his glory
> Will come in his pow'r in the beautiful day.
>
> Then pure and supernal, our friendship eternal,
> With Jesus we'll live and his counsels obey
> Until ev'ry nation will join in salvation
> And worship the Lord of the beautiful day.
>
> Beautiful day of peace and rest,
> Bright be thy dawn from east to west.
> Hail to thine earliest welcome ray,
> Beautiful, bright, millennial day.[20]

Gathering All Things in One

Ancient and modern scripture affirms that a significant part of the drama we know as the gathering of Israel will be millennial. We have witnessed miracles as the gospel has made its way into many parts of the earth, but the greatest miracles lie ahead. A major conversion of the Jews—the birth of a nation under their Head, Jesus the Messiah—will take place when he appears on the Mount of Olives (see D&C 45:48–53; Zechariah 12:9–10; 13:6).

Elders and sisters and righteous couples will, in addition, be the means of delivering the message of salvation to men and women throughout the globe. We expect that soon our missionaries will enter into lands wherein pockets of Israelites will be baptized and confirmed and where patriarchs will declare their lineage through such tribes as Issachar, Zebulun, Gad, Asher, and Naphtali. Further, during the time preceding and following our Lord's return in glory, we anticipate that millions of those not of the lineal descent of Jacob will receive the glad tidings of the Restoration, come unto Christ through the saving ordinances, and be counted by adoption as sons and daughters of Abraham, Isaac, and Jacob (Abraham 2:10).[21]

Leaning heavily upon the words of an ancient prophet, possibly Zenos, Nephi recorded: "And the time cometh speedily that the righteous must be led up as calves of the stall, and *the Holy One of Israel must reign in dominion, and might, and power, and great glory. And he gathereth his children from the four quarters of the earth;* and he numbereth his sheep, and they know him; and there shall be one fold and one shepherd; and he shall feed his sheep, and in him they shall find pasture" (1 Nephi 22:24–25; emphasis added; see also 2 Nephi 30:6–18).

The Savior himself explained to the Nephites that in the Millennium "the work of the Father"—the work of gathering, the work of inviting people to come unto Christ through missionary work—will "commence at that day" (3 Nephi 21:26). How is it that the work of the gathering of Israel will commence during the Millennium, when we have been gathering the people of the Lord since the inception of the latter-day work? Simply stated, the magnitude, magnificence, breadth, and depth of the gathering—including that which will be undertaken "among all the dispersed of my people, yea, even the tribes which have been lost" (3 Nephi 21:26)—will build upon and even surpass all that had been accomplished before. It will be as though the work had just begun.

"Therefore, behold, the days come, saith the Lord, that it shall no more be said, The Lord liveth, that brought up the children of Israel out of the land of Egypt; but, The Lord liveth, that brought up the children of Israel from the land of the north, and from all the lands whither he had driven them: and I will bring them again into their land that I gave unto their fathers." And how is this great gathering to be accomplished? "Behold, I will send for many fishers, saith the Lord, and they shall fish them; and after will I send for many hunters, and they shall hunt them from every mountain, and from every hill, and out of the holes of the rocks. For mine eyes are upon all their ways" (Jeremiah 16:14–17).

Our Lord and God will govern his people from two world capitals, "for out of Zion shall go forth the law, and the word of the Lord from Jerusalem" (Isaiah 2:3). "And he shall utter his voice out of Zion"—meaning, Independence, Missouri—"and he shall speak from Jerusalem, and his voice shall be heard among all people; and it shall be a voice as the voice of many waters, and as the voice of a great thunder, which shall break down the mountains, and the valleys shall not be found" (D&C 133:21–22). In that day the latter-day David, even Jesus Christ, the true son of David, will unite Ephraim and Judah and will preside over all Israel, from one end of the earth to the other.[22] Thus will be fulfilled the divine decree: "Be subject to the powers that be, *until he reigns whose right it is to reign, and subdues all enemies under his feet*" (D&C 58:22; emphasis added).

"How long can rolling waters remain impure?" the Prophet Joseph Smith asked in Liberty Jail. "What power shall stay the heavens? As well might man stretch forth his puny arm to stop the Missouri river in its decreed course, or to turn it up stream, as to hinder the Almighty from pouring down knowledge from heaven upon the heads of the Latter-day Saints" (D&C 121:33). The Saints have been blessed beyond measure with light and truth and sacred insights, with the scriptures of the Restoration now shedding forth their resplendent rays upon a darkened and benighted world. But there is more to come—more light, more knowledge, more doctrine, more precepts. Nothing is more set and established than the eternal fact that the canon of scripture is open, flexible, and expanding.

We will yet read the sealed portion of the Book of Mormon, that panoramic vision vouchsafed to the brother of Jared in which is to be found "a revelation from God, from the beginning of the world to the ending thereof," even "all things from the foundation of the world unto the end thereof" (2 Nephi 27:7, 10). Truly in that millennial day when men and women exercise dynamic faith like unto that of the brother of Jared, the damning veil of unbelief will be rent and we will have a complete Book of Mormon (see Ether 4:7, 15).

Further, we will be privileged to search, as did Lehi, the brass plates (1 Nephi 5:17–19; Alma 37:3–4) and to become privy to details of history and doctrine found only on the large plates of Nephi. We delight in the assurance that other sacred volumes chronicling our Redeemer's ministry to the lost tribes will come forth during the Millennium (see 2 Nephi 29:13). In short, in that glorious day we will exult in truths without number found on myriad records kept chiefly by the Nephites (see Helaman 3:13–16) as well as by other scattered branches of Israel of whom we have no knowledge. Elder Neal A. Maxwell thus observed, "Today we carry convenient quadruple combinations of the scriptures, but one day, since more scriptures are coming, we may need to pull little red wagons brimful with books."[23]

The Apostle Paul taught that "in the dispensation of the fulness of times [the Lord would] gather together in one all things in Christ, both which are in heaven, and which are on earth; even in him" (Ephesians 1:10). And surely what begins as a flowing stream in our day will become a raging river during the thousand years of peace. In that day the heavens will be opened, the Saints of the Most High will enjoy pure and sweet communion with God and angels, and eternal verities will be made known constantly. The Saints will have been cleansed of sin, and their motives will have been purified; they will no longer ask amiss for that which they ought not. Thus, "in that day whatsoever any man shall ask, it shall be given unto him" (D&C 101:27). "And it shall come to pass, that before they call, I will answer; and while they are yet speaking, I will hear" (Isaiah 65:24).

During the thousand years the covenant people of Christ's church on earth will have internalized the principles of his gospel and incorporated the law of the Lord into their very being. They will then see "eye to eye" with one another and with their Lord and Master (D&C 84:98). Jeremiah recorded the words of Jehovah:

"Behold, the days come, saith the Lord, that I will make a new covenant with the house of Israel, and with the house of Judah: not according to the covenant that I made with their fathers in the day that I took them by the hand to bring them out of the land of Egypt; which my covenant they brake, although I was an husband unto them, saith the Lord: but this shall be the covenant that I will make with the house of Israel; after those days, saith the Lord, *I will put my law in their inward parts, and write it in their hearts;* and will be their God, and they shall be my people" (Jeremiah 31:31–33; emphasis added).

The people who have accepted the fulness of the gospel in that day will know their God and be constrained to obey his will and keep his commandments. "And they shall teach no more every man his neighbour, and every man his brother, saying, Know the Lord: for *they shall all know me, from the least of them unto the greatest of them,* saith the Lord: for I will forgive their iniquity, and I will remember their sin no more" (Jeremiah 31:34; emphasis added). "How is this to be done?" Joseph Smith asked. "It is to be done by this sealing power, and the other Comforter spoken of, which will be manifest by revelation."[24]

It is a day when Christ and the resurrected Saints will dwell on earth—not permanently but periodically, "when they please, or when it is necessary to govern it."[25] It is a time wherein men and women will have grown up in the Lord (see Helaman 3:21), will have cultivated the gifts of the Spirit, and will have received "a fulness of the Holy Ghost" (D&C 109:15). The Holy Ghost will have taught and sanctified them until they are prepared to come into the presence of Christ and the Father.[26] It is the day of the Second Comforter, the day when Jesus himself will dwell among Enoch's Zion (Moses 7:16), the day when the Saints whose eyes are single to the glory of God will see him (see D&C 88:67–68). Elder Bruce R. McConkie has written:

"Men will know God in the millennial day because they see him. He will teach them face to face. They will know the mysteries of his kingdom because they are caught up to the third heaven, as was Paul. They will receive the Second Comforter. The millennial day is the day of the Second Comforter, and whereas but few have been blessed with this divine association in times past, great hosts will be so blessed in times to come."[27]

The Final Battle and the End of the Earth

For a thousand years men and women on earth will live lives of quiet nobility and will bow the knee and acknowledge Jesus the Messiah as the King of Zion and the Redeemer of all humankind. As we have noted, at the beginning of the Millennium not all of earth's inhabitants will join the true church but by the end of the thousand years, all will be of one faith. Though Satan will have been dismissed from the earth by the true King of Kings, and though he will have been bound by the righteousness of the people, men and women will still have their moral agency. They will exercise the power of choice. The Prophet Joseph Smith observed that "Satan was generally blamed for the evils which we did, but if he was the cause of all our wickedness, men could not be condemned. The devil could not compel mankind to do evil; all was voluntary."[28]

Satan's final conquest of the souls of men at the end of the Millennium will be limited to mortals. Exalted, immortal beings—those who have been changed in the twinkling of an eye or those resurrected personages who minister on earth from time to time—cannot fall, cannot apostatize. Their salvation is secure. The father of lies will thus have his way only among those living during the final years of the Millennium, those who have not arrived at the age of one hundred.[29] Those who choose to reject the Lord and his plan at this late date do so against the light of heaven; they in essence say that the sun does not shine while they see it. They are thus consigned hereafter to a kingdom of no glory as "sons of perdition."[30]

"Michael, the seventh angel, even the archangel, shall gather together his armies, even the hosts of heaven. And the devil shall gather together his armies; even the hosts of hell, and shall come up to battle against Michael and his armies. And then cometh the battle of the great God"—known also as the battle of Gog and

Magog[31]—"and the devil and his armies shall be cast away into their own place, that they shall not have power over the saints any more at all" (D&C 88:112–14).

At the end of the thousand years, after the battle of Gog and Magog, we come to that time known as "the end of the earth" (D&C 88:101; Joseph Smith–Matthew 1:55), the final cleansing and celestialization of the planet. Having been baptized by water in the days of Noah and confirmed, or baptized by fire, at the time of the Second Coming, the earth will pass through the equivalent of a death and a resurrection. It will become a glorified celestial orb, inasmuch as it will have filled "the measure of its creation" (D&C 88:25). The earth will then be a fit abode for the true and faithful, "that bodies who are of the celestial kingdom may possess it forever and ever; for, for this intent was it made and created, and for this intent are they sanctified" (D&C 88:20). The revelations assert of those who qualify for exaltation in eternity: "They are they who are the church of the Firstborn"—meaning, those who qualify for the blessings of the Firstborn, the right to inherit, possess, and receive equally as joint heirs with Christ all that the Father has. "They are they into whose hands the Father has given all things—They are they who are priests and kings," priestesses and queens, "who have received of his fulness, and of his glory. . . . Wherefore, as it is written, they are gods, even the sons [and daughters] of God" (D&C 76:54–56, 58).

Unlike so many in the religious world, Latter-day Saints anticipate celestial life on a material world. Elder Orson Pratt eloquently and powerfully made this point:

"A Saint who is one in deed and truth, does not look for an immaterial heaven, but he expects a heaven with lands, houses, cities, vegetation, rivers, and animals; with thrones, temples, palaces, kings, princes, priests, and angels; with food, raiment, musical instruments, etc., all of which are material. Indeed, *the Saints' heaven is a redeemed, glorified, celestial, material creation, inhabited by glorified material beings, male and female, organized into families,* embracing all the relationships of husbands and wives, parents and children, where sorrow, crying, pain, and death will be known no more. Or to speak still more definitely, *this earth, when glorified, is the Saints' eternal heaven. On it they expect to live, with body, parts, and holy passions; on it they expect to move and have their being;* to eat, drink, converse, worship, sing, play on musical instruments, engage in joyful, innocent, social amusements, visit neighboring towns and neighboring worlds; *indeed, matter and its qualities and properties are the only beings or things with which they expect to associate.* . . . Materiality is indelibly stamped upon the very heaven of heavens, upon all the eternal creations; it is the very essence of all existence."[32]

Those who seek to prepare themselves for what lies ahead and who have taken the Holy Spirit for their guide attempt to view things as they are now in terms of things as they will be. One day things will change. Goodness and honesty and integrity will be the order of the day; morality and decency will characterize men and women across the globe. In that sense, we look forward to the great millennial day. Though the Saints will be required to pass through many tight places, though trials and difficulties will abound on every side, though disease and death and despair will be rampant prior to the Lord's coming in glory, yet we rejoice in the fact that one day the King of Kings and Lord of Lords will take control of things, and a new day will dawn.

"For I, the Almighty, have laid my hands upon the nations, to scourge them for their wickedness. And plagues shall go forth, and they shall not be taken from the earth until I have completed my work, which shall be cut short in righteousness—until all shall know me, who remain, even from the least unto the greatest, and shall be filled with the knowledge of the Lord, and shall see eye to eye" (D&C 84:96–98). "And again, verily I say unto you, the coming of the Lord draweth nigh, and it overtaketh the world as a thief in the night—therefore, gird up your loins, that you may be the children of light, and that day shall not overtake you as a thief" (D&C 106:4–5).

The faithful will not be surprised. The children of light—those who honor their covenants and are true to their trusts, who seek for and cultivate the spirit of revelation—will be in a position to read the signs of the times and be prepared for the great and terrible day of the Lord. They will abide the day, be caught up to meet their Master, and feel peace and confidence in his presence.

Conclusion

THE OVERARCHING MESSAGES OF JOHN'S REVELATION

Even if we are uncertain as to the meanings of many of the unusual symbols in the Apocalypse, we can grasp and appreciate the overarching messages of this book of holy scripture, some of which follow.

1. Those Saints who overcome the world will receive from Christ the supernal rewards of the faithful: they will "eat of the tree of life," which means they will gain eternal life (2:7; see Alma 32:41); they will not be overcome by "the second death" (2:11); they will come to know all things, even as God does (see 2:17; D&C 130:9–11); they will gain power over many kingdoms and rule "with the word of God" (JST, Revelation 2:26–27), even as Christ, who is "the bright and morning star" (JST, Revelation 22:16); they will be adorned in white, the robes of righteousness (see 3:4; 19:8); they will have the name of God written upon them (3:12); they will be gods;[1] and they will sit with Christ on his throne, even as Christ also overcame and sits on the throne of the Father (see 3:21; see also D&C 93:20).

2. Jesus Christ, who is "the Lion of the tribe of Juda, the Root of David," has power to loose the seals on the record of men's dealings on earth (see 5:5). In other words, the Master knows the end from the beginning—he knows what was, what is, and what is to

111

be. His is the eternal perspective, and we can trust in and rely on his all-knowing and all-loving wisdom in orchestrating the events of our lives.

3. "Worthy is the Lamb that was slain to receive power, and riches, and wisdom, and strength, and honour, and glory, and blessing" (5:12). Indeed, if any people in all the world have reason to rejoice in the Lord, it is the Latter-day Saints. When we contemplate what has been restored to earth—knowledge and power and gifts abounding—we ought to lift our voices to heaven and exult with the Revelator, "Alleluia: for the Lord God omnipotent reigneth" (19:6).

4. The war that began in heaven continues on earth (12:7–10) and will be waged until the Savior returns in glory. Many in our day are afflicted with the same poison that afflicts Lucifer and his followers—they are "accuser[s] of our brethren" (12:10). But the faithful overcome dissidence and opposition and persecution "by the blood of the Lamb, and by the word of their testimony," for "they [love] not their lives unto the death" (12:11).

5. Despite the rising tide of wickedness, the Lord saw fit to restore the fulness of his gospel. John "saw another angel fly in the midst of heaven, having the everlasting gospel to preach unto them that dwell on the earth, and to every nation, and kindred, and tongue, and people" (14:6). President Gordon B. Hinckley testified:

"That angel has come. His name is Moroni. His is a voice speaking from the dust, bringing another witness of the living reality of the Lord Jesus Christ.

"We have not as yet carried the gospel to every nation, kindred, tongue, and people. But we have made great strides. We have gone wherever we are permitted to go. God is at the helm and doors will be opened by His power according to His divine will. Of that I am confident. Of that I am certain."[2]

6. All people will be judged by their works out of the books

that are written on earth and in heaven (see 20:12–13; see also D&C 128:6–7). "He that overcometh shall inherit all things; and I will be his God, and he shall be my son" (21:7). The faithful will become kings and priests, queens and priestesses unto God forever (see 1:5–6; 5:10; 20:6).

7. Wickedness will increase, malevolence will multiply, and the forces of evil will cover the globe. But the great and abominable church will eventually fall, and Satanic influences will be no more (17–19). Eventually good will triumph over evil on this earth. A day of righteousness will be ushered in at the time of our Savior's return in glory. Satan will be bound, and the work of God will go forward without distraction for a thousand years. At the end of that glorious era, the devil will be loosed for a little season, but he and his minions will be defeated by the powers of God, and a final cleansing will take place. The earth will then become the celestial kingdom (21–22; D&C 88:17–20).

The Prophet Joseph Smith taught, "The book of Revelation is one of the plainest books God ever caused to be written."[3] Some of us who struggle with understanding this rather esoteric book of scripture might be prone to suggest that such a point of view is appropriate for one who, like the Prophet, has essentially seen and experienced what John the Revelator saw and experienced. I sense, however, that Joseph had reference to the key themes, the unmistakable principles that are found in Revelation, more than the seemingly endless symbolic details. We can all understand these central messages. We can, like former-day Saints, watch and be ready. We can be vigilant, ever alert to evil in all its diverse forms. We can take heart that the God of heaven is in charge, that he presides over the affairs of men and women, and that divine justice and pardoning mercy will yet deliver and reward the Saints.

Chart 1

THE ORGANIZATION OF THE BOOK OF REVELATION

I. Prologue (1:1–20)

   a. Introduction (1:1–3)

   b. Salutation (1:4–8)

   c. The first vision (1:9–20)

II. The Letters to the Churches (2:1–3:22)

   a. Ephesus (2:1–7)

   b. Smyrna (2:8–11)

   c. Pergamos (2:12–17)

   d. Thyatira (2:18–29)

   e. Sardis (3:1–6)

   f. Philadelphia (3:7–13)

   g. Laodicea (3:14–22)

III. A Vision of Heaven (4:1–11)

IV. The Seven Seals (5:1–8:5)

   a. The unopened book (5:1–5)

   b. The Lion of the tribe of Juda (5:5–14)

   c. The first seal (6:1–2)

   d. The second seal (6:3–4)

   e. The third seal (6:5–6)

    f. The fourth seal (6:7–8)

    g. The fifth seal (6:9–11)

    h. The sixth seal (6:12–17)

    i. An interlude (7:1–17)

    j. The seventh seal (8:1–5)

V. The Seven Trumpets (8:6–11:19)

    a. The first trumpet (8:6–7)

    b. The second trumpet (8:8–9)

    c. The third trumpet (8:10–11)

    d. The fourth trumpet (8:12)

    e. The eagle (8:13)

    f. The fifth trumpet (9:1–12)

    g. The sixth trumpet (9:13–21)

    h. An interlude (10:1–11:14)

    i. The seventh trumpet (11:15–19)

VI. The Seven Significant Signs (12:1–14:20)

    a. The woman clothed with the sun (12:1–6)

    b. Satan cast out (12:7–12)

    c. War between Satan and the woman and her son (12:13–17)

    d. The beast from the sea (13:1–10)

    e. The beast from the earth (13:11–18)

    f. The Lamb on Mount Zion (14:1–5)

    g. The harvest of the earth (14:6–20)

VII. The Seven Last Plagues (15:1–16:21)

    a. Preliminaries (15:1–8)

    b. The first vial (16:1–2)

    c. The second vial (16:3)

    d. The third vial (16:4–7)

    e. The fourth vial (16:8–9)

    f. The fifth vial (16:10–11)

    g. The sixth vial (16:12–16)

    h. The seventh vial (16:17–21)

VIII. The Triumph of Almighty God (17:1–20:15)

    a. The judgment of the great whore (17:1–18)

    b. The judgment of Babylon (18:1–19:6)

    c. The marriage of the Lamb (19:7–10)

    d. The final victory (19:11–20:15)

IX. A New Heaven and a New Earth (21:1–22:5)

    a. "God . . . with them" (21:1–4)

    b. Separation between good and evil (21:5–8)

    c. The holy city (21:9–21)

    d. "No night there" (21:22–22:5)

X. Epilogue (22:6–21)

Chart 2

A CHRONOLOGICAL OUTLINE
OF THE BOOK OF REVELATION

The Drama of the Forces of Good (Christ) and its Historical
Struggle with the Forces of Evil (Anti-Christ)

BEFORE JOHN'S DAY	JOHN'S DAY AND TIME (ABOUT A.D. 90–110)	LATTER DAYS (AFTER JOHN)
	REVELATION 1–3 Problems the Saints were having—seven churches	
	REVELATION 4–5 Revelation 4—vision of God's majesty Revelation 5—vision of Christ's majesty 1. Twenty-four elders 2. Sea of glass 3. Four beasts (eyes and wings) 4. The Lamb opens the sealed book (Christ is the God of this world)	

BEFORE JOHN'S DAY	JOHN'S DAY AND TIME (ABOUT A.D. 90–110)	LATTER DAYS (AFTER JOHN)
REVELATION 6:1–8 Four horses of the Apocalypse. John is allowed to peek into the seven seals of each book. Each seal represents 1,000 years of the earth's temporal history. Each horse and rider represent some part of the historical drama between good and evil.	**REVELATION 6:9–11** The "fifth seal" tells of the crisis John and his people were suffering.	**REVELATION 6:12–17** The "sixth seal" is the last dispensation, the last days, the "great day" of the Lord.
		REVELATION 7–9 Continues showing events of last days, the final plagues to be poured out, and so forth. 1. Four angels 2. Angel from the East 3. 144,000 sealed 4. Seventh seal is opened 5. Destroying angels begin
	REVELATION 10 Vision to John about eating a book (sweet and bitter). The book represents a future mission of John the Beloved.	**REVELATION 11** 1. A "spiritual temple" of God's people 2. Gentiles will trample the Holy City for forty-two months 3. Two witnesses or prophets
PREMORTALITY		
What is the origin of evil? **REVELATION 12** There is a war in heaven. Satan and his angels are cast down to earth.	**REVELATION 12** The devil tries to destroy the Church. The Church flees for a set period of time—1,260 days (JST, Revelation 12:6 says "years").	

BEFORE JOHN'S DAY	JOHN'S DAY AND TIME (ABOUT A.D. 90–110)	LATTER DAYS (AFTER JOHN)
	REVELATION 13 John now describes the present evil in his day: 1. Two beasts, one from sea and one from land (emperor or Rome and its imperial priesthood) 2. Beast has one head seriously wounded 3. Beast overcomes Saints for "forty-two months" 4. Beast is a man; his number is 666	**REVELATION 14–16** An interlude of righteousness and harvest in the last days: 1. 144,000 selected 2. Angel restores gospel 3. Final destruction by angels 4. Last great battle—Armageddon
	REVELATION 17–18 More elaboration on the evil of John's day: 1. Roma, the goddess of Rome, is depicted 2. Roman empire and emperors are depicted 3. Seven heads—seven hills of Rome and seven emperors 4. One head "was," "is not," "yet is" 5. Corruption and fall of spiritual wickedness—"Babylon"	**REVELATION 19** 1. Final destruction of evil 2. The bridegroom comes for the bride 3. Rewards and punishments
		MILLENNIUM
		REVELATION 20–22 1. Satan bound 2. Millennium 3. Battle of Gog and Magog 4. Judgments 5. New Jerusalem 6. Paradisiacal Earth

NOTES

Introduction:
Making Sense of John's Revelation

1. See also Joseph Smith, *Teachings*, 191.

2. Smith, *Teachings*, 247.

3. Smith, *Teachings*, 220.

4. Smith, *Teachings*, 287, 291.

5. Romney, "A Glorious Promise," 2.

6. Smith, *Teachings*, 287–94.

7. Smith, *Teachings*, 289; emphasis added.

8. See McConkie, *Doctrinal New Testament Commentary*, 3:476–85.

Part One: Examining the Book of Revelation
1. Prologue (1:1–20)

1. Joseph Smith, *Teachings*, 220; emphasis added.

2. "Rejoice, the Lord Is King!" *Hymns*, no. 66.

2. The Letters to the Churches (2:1–3:22)

1. Benson, "The Great Commandment," 4.

2. See Lee, *Ye Are the Light of the World*, 211.

3. McConkie, *Doctrinal New Testament Commentary*, 3:446.

4. "Nicolaitans," *Anchor Bible Dictionary*, 4:1106–7.

5. See "Nicolaitans," *Anchor Bible Dictionary*, 4:1107.

6. McConkie, *Mormon Doctrine*, 409.

7. McConkie, *Doctrinal New Testament Commentary*, 3:460.

3. A Vision of Heaven (4:1–11)

1. Joseph Smith, *Teachings*, 292.

4. The Seven Seals (5:1–8:5)

1. See Joseph Smith, *Teachings*, 318.
2. Wright, *After You Believe*, 88–90; emphasis in original.
3. Edward Stevenson, *Reminiscences of Joseph, the Prophet, and the Coming Forth of the Book of Mormon* (1893), 6; in Andrus and Andrus, *They Knew the Prophet*, 85.
4. See Smith, *Teachings*, 321.
5. Smith, *Teachings*, 321.
6. Whitney, in Conference Report, April 1929, 110.
7. Packer, "Our Moral Environment," 68.

5. The Seven Trumpets (8:6–11:19)

1. See McConkie, *Doctrinal New Testament Commentary*, 3:499.
2. *New International Version Study Bible*, Revelation 8:13.
3. See McConkie, *Doctrinal New Testament Commentary*, 3:501.
4. See McConkie, *Doctrinal New Testament Commentary*, 3:505.
5. See also Joseph Smith, *Teachings*, 158.
6. McConkie, *Doctrinal New Testament Commentary*, 3:509; emphasis added; see also McConkie, *Millennial Messiah*, 390.
7. This appears to be the same massive earthquake described in Revelation 16:16–20 and in Doctrine and Covenants 133:21–24; see also D&C 45:48.

6. The Seven Significant Signs (12:1–14:20)

1. Taylor, in *Journal of Discourses*, 18:137.
2. Joseph Smith, *Teachings*, 357.
3. Smith, *Teachings*, 289.
4. Most commentaries on Revelation refer to this interpretation. For a Latter-day Saint treatment, see Durham, "Revelation."
5. Morris, *Revelation*, 169.
6. Pratt, in *Journal of Discourses*, 4:242–43.
7. McConkie, *Doctrinal New Testament Commentary*, 3:526–27.
8. See Joseph Fielding Smith, *Doctrines of Salvation*, 1:174.

7. The Seven Last Plagues (15:1–16:21)

1. Morris, *Revelation*, 191–92.
2. McConkie, *Millennial Messiah*, 476, 484–85.

8. The Triumph of Almighty God (17:1–20:15)

1. McConkie, *Doctrinal New Testament Commentary*, 3:552–53.
2. Morris, *Revelation*, 204.
3. See also Joseph Smith, *Teachings*, 101.
4. See Cannon, in *Journal of Discourses*, 16:119–20.
5. Smith, *Teachings*, 268.
6. Smith, *Teachings*, 280.
7. Oaks, *With Full Purpose of Heart*, 75.

9. A New Heaven and a New Earth (21:1–22:5)

1. Morris, *Revelation*, 244.
2. Morris, *Revelation*, 249.

Part Two: The Second Coming of Christ
Questions and Answers

1. See also Joseph Smith, *Teachings*, 101.
2. Ballard, "'When Shall These Things Be?'" 56; emphasis added.
3. *Times and Seasons*, 4:109.
4. Pratt, in *Journal of Discourses*, 15:365–66.
5. Penrose, *Millennial Star* 21, 582–83.
6. Smith, *Teachings*, 157.
7. Joseph Fielding Smith, *Progress of Man*, 481–82; see also Joseph Fielding Smith, *Way to Perfection*, 288–91.
8. McConkie, *Millennial Messiah*, 582, 584.
9. Joseph Fielding Smith, *Signs of the Times*, 42.
10. Smith, *Signs of the Times*, 41.
11. Joseph Smith, *Teachings*, 301; see also 297, 305.
12. Romney, "The Light Shineth," 75.
13. See McConkie, *Millennial Messiah*, 240–41.
14. See Smith, *Teachings*, 308.
15. See also McConkie, *Millennial Messiah*, 214–17, 325–27.
16. Joseph Smith, *History of the Church*, 4:540.
17. McConkie, in Palmer, *Expanding Church*, 141–42.
18. Faust, "Untroubled Faith," 71.
19. Packer, "'To Be Learned Is Good If . . . ,'" 73.
20. Lee, "Admonitions," 106.
21. McConkie, *Millennial Messiah*, 635.
22. "The Morning Breaks," *Hymns*, no. 1.

Part Three: The Millennium

1. Pratt, in *Journal of Discourses*, 16:319; emphasis added.

2. Benson, *Teachings*, 18.

3. McConkie, *Millennial Messiah*, 627.

4. See McConkie, *Millennial Messiah*, 627–28, 636, 647; see also McConkie, *New Witness*, 588.

5. See Joseph Smith, *Teachings*, 191.

6. McConkie, *Millennial Messiah*, 644–45.

7. Young, in *Journal of Discourses*, 11:275.

8. Young, in *Journal of Discourses*, 2:316; emphasis added.

9. Young, in *Journal of Discourses*, 12:274.

10. Joseph Fielding Smith, *Doctrines of Salvation*, 3:64.

11. See Smith, *Doctrines of Salvation*, 3:63–64.

12. Joseph Smith, *Teachings*, 269.

13. McConkie, *Millennial Messiah*, 652.

14. Cannon, *Gospel Truth*, 70; emphasis added.

15. See Smith, *Teachings*, 308.

16. Woodruff, in *Journal of Discourses*, 13:327.

17. Joseph F. Smith, "Redemption Beyond the Grave," 146–47.

18. Young, in *Journal of Discourses*, 3:372; emphasis added.

19. McConkie, *Millennial Messiah*, 673–74.

20. "The Day Dawn Is Breaking," *Hymns*, no. 52.

21. See Joseph Smith, *Teachings*, 149–50.

22. See McConkie, *Millennial Messiah*, 602–11; see also McConkie, *New Witness*, 518.

23. Maxwell, *Wonderful Flood of Light*, 18.

24. Smith, *Teachings*, 149.

25. Smith, *Teachings*, 268.

26. See Joseph Smith, *Words of Joseph Smith*, 14–15.

27. McConkie, *Millennial Messiah*, 682.

28. Smith, *Teachings*, 187.

29. See Pratt, in *Journal of Discourses*, 16:322; see also Joseph Fielding Smith, *Doctrines of Salvation*, 2:56–57.

30. McConkie, *New Witness*, 652.

31. See Smith, *Teachings*, 280.

32. Pratt, *Masterful Discourses*, 62–63; emphasis added.

Conclusion:
The Overarching Messages of John's Revelation

1. See also Pratt, in *Journal of Discourses*, 14:242–43.

2. Hinckley, "Stay the Course," 70–71.

3. Joseph Smith, *Teachings*, 290.

SOURCES

Anchor Bible Dictionary. Edited by David Noel Friedman. 6 vols. New York: Doubleday, 1992.

Andrus, Hyrum L. and Helen Mae Andrus. *They Knew the Prophet.* Salt Lake City: Bookcraft, 1974.

Ballard, M. Russell. "When Shall These Things Be?" *Ensign,* December 1996, 56–61.

Benson, Ezra Taft. "The Great Commandment—Love the Lord." *Ensign,* May 1988, 4–6.

———. *The Teachings of Ezra Taft Benson.* Salt Lake City: Bookcraft, 1988.

Callister, Tad R. *The Inevitable Apostasy and the Promised Restoration.* Salt Lake City: Deseret Book, 2006.

Cannon, George Q. *Gospel Truth.* Compiled by Jerreld L. Newquist. 2 vols. in 1. Salt Lake City: Deseret Book, 1987.

Conference Reports of The Church of Jesus Christ of Latter-day Saints. Salt Lake City: The Church of Jesus Christ of Latter-day Saints, 1898–.

Durham, Reed C. "Revelation: The Plainest Book Ever Written." *New Era,* May 1973, 21–27.

Faust, James E. "An Untroubled Faith." *Ensign,* March 1988, 69–72.

Hinckley, Gordon B. "Stay the Course—Keep the Faith." *Ensign,* November 1995, 70–72.

Hymns of The Church of Jesus Christ of Latter-day Saints. Salt Lake City: The Church of Jesus Christ of Latter-day Saints, 1985.

Journal of Discourses. 26 vols. London: Latter-day Saints' Book Depot, 1854–86.

Lee, Harold B. "Admonitions for the Priesthood of God." *Ensign,* January 1973, 104–8.

———. *Ye Are the Light of the World.* Salt Lake City: Deseret Book, 1973.

Maxwell, Neal A. *A Wonderful Flood of Light.* Salt Lake City: Bookcraft, 1990.

McConkie, Bruce R. *Doctrinal New Testament Commentary.* 3 vols. Salt Lake City: Bookcraft, 1965–73.

———. *The Millennial Messiah: The Second Coming of the Son of Man.* Salt Lake City: Deseret Book, 1982.

———. *Mormon Doctrine.* 2d ed. Salt Lake City: Bookcraft, 1966.

———. *A New Witness for the Articles of Faith.* Salt Lake City: Deseret Book, 1985.

Millennial Star. Liverpool: The Church of Jesus Christ of Latter-day Saints, 1840–1970.

Morris, Leon. *Revelation: An Introduction and Commentary.* The Tyndale New Testament Commentaries. Downers Grove, Illinois: IVP Academic, 1987.

The New International Version Study Bible. Grand Rapids, Michigan: Zondervan, 1985.

Oaks, Dallin H. *With Full Purpose of Heart.* Salt Lake City: Deseret Book, 2002.

Packer, Boyd K. "Our Moral Environment." *Ensign,* May 1992, 66–68.

———. "'To Be Learned Is Good If . . .'" *Ensign,* November 1992, 71–73.

Palmer, Spencer J. *The Expanding Church.* Salt Lake City: Deseret Book, 1978.

Pratt, Orson. *Masterful Discourses of Orson Pratt.* Salt Lake City: Bookcraft, 1962.

Romney, Marion G. "A Glorious Promise." *Ensign,* January 1981, 2–3.

———. "'The Light Shineth.'" *Ensign,* December 1971, 75–77.

Smith, Joseph. *History of The Church of Jesus Christ of Latter-day Saints.*

Edited by B. H. Roberts. 2d ed. rev. 7 vols. Salt Lake City: The Church of Jesus Christ of Latter-day Saints, 1932–51.

———. *Teachings of the Prophet Joseph Smith.* Selected by Joseph Fielding Smith. Salt Lake City: Deseret Book, 1976.

———. *The Words of Joseph Smith: Contemporary Accounts of the Nauvoo Discourses.* Edited by Andrew F. Ehat and Lyndon W. Cook. Provo, Utah: BYU Religious Studies Center, 1980.

Smith, Joseph F. "Redemption Beyond the Grave." *Improvement Era* 5, no. 2 (December 1901): 145–47.

Smith, Joseph Fielding. *Doctrines of Salvation.* Compiled by Bruce R. McConkie. 3 vols. Salt Lake City: Bookcraft, 1954–56.

———. *The Progress of Man.* Salt Lake City: Deseret Book, 1964.

———. *The Signs of the Times.* Salt Lake City: Deseret Book, 1942.

———. *The Way to Perfection.* Salt Lake City: Deseret Book, 1970.

Times and Seasons. 6 vols. Nauvoo, Illinois: The Church of Jesus Christ of Latter-day Saints, 1839–46.

Wright, N. T. *After You Believe: Why Christian Character Matters.* New York: Harper One, 2010.

INDEX

ABOUT THE AUTHOR

Robert L. Millet is Abraham O. Smoot University Professor and professor of ancient scripture at Brigham Young University. He earned his master's degree in psychology from BYU and his PhD in religious studies from Florida State University. Brother Millet has served in the Church as a bishop, stake president, temple ordinance worker, and a member of the Church Materials Evaluation Committee. He and his wife, Shauna, have six children and ten grandchildren and reside in Orem, Utah.